Praise for *Lovestruck*

"*Lovestruck* is a refreshing, beautiful, and biblical love letter for the mind, heart, soul, and body of a couple. Sharon Jaynes gives us the WHY love, marriage, intimacy, and sex are a powerful gift from God and HOW we all can cultivate value and appreciation of this precious gift, then apply these truths to unwrap the gift of love in our own marriages."

—Pam and Bill Farrel, bestselling authors of *Men Are Like Waffles, Women Are Like Spaghetti* and *Red Hot Monogamy*

"With winsome vulnerability and endearing honesty, Sharon delivers a holistic tool for understanding, appreciating, and navigating God's gift that is marriage. Intentionally biblical and thoughtfully practical."

—J.D. Greear, Ph.D., 62nd president, the Southern Baptist Convention; pastor, The Summit Church, Raleigh-Durham, NC; author of *Above All*

"Want to know what God has to say about marriage and sex? (Psst . . . He thinks it's a great idea!) On the pages of this book, Sharon shows us how to pursue the love and intimacy our hearts crave by digging into and understanding the passionate lifelong love between one man and one woman found in the Song of Solomon. Ready to take your marriage to the next level? Read this book!"

—Jill Savage, author of *No More Perfect Marriages* and *Is There Really Sex After Kids?*

"*Lovestruck* is a must-read for any woman who wants to revive and keep romance alive in her marriage for years to come! This deep dive into the book of the Song of Solomon unpacks the rich, relevant, and even racy truths that remind us of not only the beginnings of love and romance, but also the journey toward oneness that takes place over years of marriage. In a time when our culture is shouting that it's normal to 'fall out of love,' this is a refreshing reminder that the pursuit of each other can grow and, with time, not just fade away. *Lovestruck* is authentic and relatable and full of practical ways to make your marriage and romance truly thrive!"

—Meg and David Robbins,
president and CEO, FamilyLife

"My husband has always been a big fan of the Song of Solomon for its romantic content. Now after reading *Lovestruck*, I am too! Sharon Jaynes has done a masterful job in explaining this mysterious book. Some pages made me cry, other pages made me want to whirl around like a giddy schoolgirl in love. If you want to return to the passion of first love—and enjoy the sweetness of lasting love—read this book! You (and your husband) will be glad you did."

—Arlene Pellicane, speaker and author
of *31 Days to a Happy Husband*

Lovestruck

Lovestruck

Discovering God's Design for Romance,
Marriage, & Sexual Intimacy
from the Song of Solomon

SHARON JAYNES

NELSON BOOKS
An Imprint of Thomas Nelson

Published in Nashville, Tennessee, by Nelson Books, an imprint of Thomas Nelson. Nelson Books and Thomas Nelson are registered trademarks of HarperCollins Christian Publishing, Inc.

Thomas Nelson titles may be purchased in bulk for educational, business, fund-raising, or sales promotional use. For information, please e-mail SpecialMarkets@ThomasNelson.com.

Library of Congress Cataloging-in-Publication Data

Names: Jaynes, Sharon, author.
Title: Lovestruck: discovering God's design for romance, marriage, and sexual intimacy from the Song of Solomon / Sharon Jaynes.
Description: Nashville, Tennessee: Nelson Books, an imprint of Thomas Nelson. Nelson, [2019] | Includes bibliographical references.
Identifiers: LCCN 2018048536 (print) | LCCN 2018051941 (ebook) | ISBN 9781400209668 (e-book) | ISBN 9781400209644 (pbk.)
Subjects: LCSH: Bible. Song of Solomon—Criticism, interpretation, etc. Marriage—Biblical teaching. | Christian women—Religious life.
Classification: LCC BS1485.52 (ebook) | LCC BS1485.52 .J39 2019 (print) | DDC 223/.906—dc23
LC record available at https://lccn.loc.gov/2018048536

Printed in the United States of America

19 20 21 22 23 LSC 10 9 8 7 6 5 4 3 2 1

To Steven and Emily
What a joy watching you continue the legacy of lifelong love through the covenant of marriage

Contents

Introduction

It was time to clean out my attic, at least some of it. I pulled out several pieces of furniture to take to a consignment store, three lamps to take to a nonprofit thrift shop, and many items that went straight to the trash. In one corner sat memorabilia we'd saved from Steve's parents' attic years ago. That's when I saw it. Tucked under a dusty old wing chair hid a tattered box. I pulled back the musty flaps and slid out what appeared to be a letter. I gasped as I lifted the frail envelope and unfolded sacred words from my husband's dad, Bruce, to the petite beauty "with chestnut hair, a Coke-bottle figure, and plenty of book smarts."

My husband's parents grew up in the mountains of North Carolina in the sleepy little town of Waynesville. Back in the 1940s, high school only went through eleventh grade, with an optional twelfth for those who wanted to continue their studies. Since Mary Ellen was one grade behind him, Bruce made the decision to stay one more year . . . to continue his studies, of course.

Bruce and Mary Ellen were a striking couple. His six-foot-four-inch stature, with a muscular build and a thirty-two-inch waist, towered over Mary Ellen's five-foot-three-inch frame. No one was surprised when Bruce asked Mary Ellen to be his bride just a few days after graduation. But World War II interrupted the couple's plans. Duty called, and Bruce shipped off to the US Army training camp in Scott Field, Illinois, and then on to the Aleutian Islands in the Northern Pacific. That's when the letters began.

More than five hundred letters written over two and a half years had been stowed away in a cardboard box . . . until now. I pulled out the fragile treasures one by one and read intimate words of sacred devotion from a man head over heels in love with his high school sweetheart. The letters began as a soldier writing to the girl back home who had stolen his heart—one he pursued with pen and ink. And then about a third of the way through, the letters changed. The envelopes were no longer addressed to Mary Ellen Boone, but to Mary Ellen Jaynes.

On a crisp November afternoon in 1943, during one of Bruce's furloughs, he and Mary Ellen became husband and wife. When he went back to his station in the Aleutian Islands, the letters picked right back up where they had left off before. Seventy-four years later, I savored these pages as a celebration of commitment, loyalty, passion, and love that lasted their lifetimes. What a beautiful gift it was for me to get to witness this kind of love.

You and I have that same opportunity when we read the passionate words of a lovestruck couple in the Word of God.

The Bible opens with the marriage of a man and a woman in the garden of Eden and concludes with the marriage of Christ and the church in the New Jerusalem, letting us know that marriage and intimacy are important to God. Even Jesus' first miracle took place at a wedding in Cana where he turned water into wine. How fitting that God nestled one of the most passionate love stories of all time right in the middle of his love letter to us. Tucked in between the introspective book of Ecclesiastes and the prophetic book of Isaiah lies a work of poetry that memorializes mutual attraction, romantic love, sexual desire, and enduring marriage between a man smitten and a woman bedazzled: the Song of Solomon.

With all the resources about love and marriage available, why should we go back to this ancient piece of literature to help us as we pursue the love and intimacy our hearts crave? Because it tells us what

God has to say about marriage and sex, and not just in a smattering of verses sprinkled here and there. Eight full chapters are dedicated solely to the purpose of putting on display the passionate lifelong love between one man and one woman—a rare treasure indeed.

Many of the marriage books out today (and I've written a few of them) focus on the how-tos of building successful marriages. Tips. Tricks. Tactics. And, yes, there's going to be some of that here, but the main focus we'll bring to the Song of Solomon is not the *how* but the *why.* Why did God create man and woman to be mutually attracted to each other? Why did God go to such great lengths to fashion our bodies to desire and enjoy sexual intimacy? Why do so many marriages cool with the passage of time? Why are men and women wired so differently? Why do some couples make marriage work for a lifetime and others do not? Once we understand the *why*, then we can better apply the *how.*

The first *why* we need to tackle before we dig in to the Scripture is, why is our culture so confused about romance, sex, and marriage—especially sex?

Sex and the Culture

Sex. It has been used to sell everything from movie tickets and clothes to shampoo and corn chips. Advertisers refer to the sleek and seductive allure of certain cars as sexy. They tout the tingly freshness of a certain toothpaste that will supposedly make the opposite sex want to lean in for a kiss. Commercials show a man's electric razor enticingly sliding over his chiseled jaw, promising irresistible sexual attraction. Sex in advertising started back in 1885 when a manufacturer of facial soap included in the soap's packaging trading cards with provocative images of the day's most popular female stars.[1] And from that time until now, advertisers agree: sex sells.

One day I was at a clothing store geared toward teens and young adults, one where the store owners had obviously decided that posters with shirtless young guys sells shirts. At the checkout counter sat a bowl of candy with a sign that read Sexy Mints. I wanted to say, "Excuse me, what makes these mints sexy? Can you please tell me?" But I didn't want to embarrass the teenager with me, who was looking a bit nervous. I could see him holding his breath as I eyed the sign. It was really difficult to keep my mouth shut.

Everywhere we turn these days we're hit with a barrage of sexual images attacking our senses. Television, movies, the Internet, shopping-mall window dressings, music lyrics, and the list goes on. By the time a teen graduates from high school, he or she will have seen no fewer than fourteen thousand references to sex on television.[2] And this pervasiveness follows us into adulthood. In fact, pornography is now a $10 billion industry—taking in more money than Major League Baseball, the NBA, and the NFL combined.[3] It's no wonder that our sex-saturated culture is so confused and misguided. Jesus said, "The thief comes only to steal and kill and destroy" (John 10:10), and he has clearly pulled out all the stops to destroy God's intent for sexual intimacy and marriage.

I don't want you to get me wrong here. I don't think sex is a bad thing. God created sex, and he considers what he made "very good" (Genesis 1:31). I believe the problem is not that our culture focuses on sex too much but that it values sex too little. Sex is meant to be so much more than a physical act of carnal urges. Sex was created to be a sacred union between a husband and wife, designed by a holy, ingenious, and immensely generous God. When we understand the weighty worth and sacred significance of sex, we treasure and enjoy it even more.

God intended sex to be a gift enjoyed in the safe boundaries of marriage. We all know that marriage itself has taken a hit in the past fifty years. Only half of Americans ages eighteen and older were married in 2016, which is a decrease of nine percentage points over the past quarter century.[4] Young adults are getting married later now, and even when they do, they face skepticism about whether lifelong marriages are even possible. With the delay of marriage, the doubt of its longevity, and the devaluing of physical intimacy, many in our culture have traded in the invaluable treasure of marital lovemaking for dime-store hook-up sex. But it doesn't have to be this way.

> The problem is not that our culture focuses on sex too much but that it values sex too little.

In contrast, the Bible boldly paints a beautiful picture of how sexual intimacy can be when we pursue love the way God purposed it to be from the beginning. It gives us principles to practice in order to experience the most fulfilling marriage possible, including guidance for sexual fulfillment at its best. God isn't a spoilsport who wants to keep people from having sex, but a loving, masterful Creator who wants husbands and wives to experience passionate physical intimacy for a lifetime.

I was sitting beside a twenty-three-year-old man in an airplane one day, and we bantered back and forth about where we were from and what we did back home. The conversation eventually swung around to my work as a writer.

"What are you working on now?" he asked.

Heat crept up my neck as I cautiously replied, "I'm writing a book on marriage and sex based on the Song of Solomon in the Bible."

Without batting an eye he replied, "I'm so glad you're doing that. My generation is so mixed up when it comes to sex. They hook up with people they barely know. By the time they get married, they've slept with so many different people that sex has lost its specialness. We need to know how to do it the right way."

That was not what I had been expecting to hear from this handsome young man beside me. But I will tell you this: after our conversation I attacked this subject with a new vigor and verve.

Literal or Allegorical?

Are you excited to discover what God has to say about this important subject? I am, but before we delve into the Song of Solomon, let's answer the question many have asked through the centuries: Is this book literal or allegorical? Because the verses are so erotically sensual, many early Bible scholars concluded that the book must be an allegory—a picture of Christ's love for the church. Modern theologians, such as R. C. Sproul, suggest that ancient scholars were so embarrassed by the sensual imagery of the Song that they tried to spiritualize it.[5] I have read many of those early writings, and a lot of them are quite a stretch. I suspect that the centuries-old writers just couldn't bring themselves to take the book at face value, so they interpreted it as an allegory.

One early commentator said the woman's breasts in the Song represent the Old and the New Testaments.[6] Another said her breasts refer to faith and love.[7] But it is hard to spiritualize verses such as, "Your stature is like that of the palm, and your breasts like clusters of fruit. I said, 'I will climb the palm tree; I will take hold of its fruit'" (Song 7:7–8). That's pretty straightforward. I believe, along with many modern theologians, that the Song of Solomon is to be taken literally. It's a book about romantic love between a man and a woman. It's a celebration of courtship, romance, marriage, and sexual intimacy. And we have a lot to learn.

While we're looking at the Song literally, the Bible *does* tell us that marriage is a reflection of the relationship between Christ and his church. The book of Revelation says, "Let us rejoice and be glad and give him glory! For the wedding of the Lamb [Jesus] has come, and his bride [the church] has made herself ready" (19:7). John had a vision of "the Holy City, the new Jerusalem, coming down out of heaven from God, prepared as a bride beautifully dressed for her husband" (21:2). And perhaps the most compelling reference is Paul's letter to the

Ephesians, which explicitly compares the marriage between a husband and wife to the union of Christ and his church (Ephesians 5:21–33).

Based on these scriptures, marriage *is* an earthly picture of the heavenly union we experience when we come to Jesus—the truest of holy matrimonies and sacred wedlock. Even the two becoming one flesh in marriage is a picture of our becoming one with Christ. And, further, the thrilling passion of sex and the otherworldliness of love point our hearts toward the embodiment of love, God himself.

So, yes, there is value in looking at concepts of love, romance, and marriage through a metaphorical lens, and, in a sense, the Song of Solomon does point us back to Jesus. But it's not because the lover (Jesus) pursues the lowly woman in the field (you and me), but because romantic love in itself is an echo of God's love for us. While we will see Jesus' reflection in the words of the beloved to his maiden in Song of Solomon, we will be looking at the passage as I believe it was intended, from a literal point of view.

The Big Surprise

Every time I teach on the Song of Solomon, women are surprised. "Is that really in the Bible?" they ask wide-eyed. Yep, right in the holy Writ. The Song is what Tim Keller calls the "barefaced rejoicing in the delights of sexual love in marriage."[8]

Some have wondered why this erotic book is included in the Bible. And why even study it at all? Primarily we study it *because it is* in Scripture. Second Timothy 3 reminds us, "All Scripture is God-breathed and is useful for teaching, rebuking, correcting and training in righteousness, so that the servant of God may be thoroughly equipped for every good work" (vv. 16–17). God intends for us to read it, learn from it, be corrected by it, and trained with it.

The Song of Solomon is unlike any other book in the Bible. It is a poem and a love song that portrays God's original intent for courtship, romance, and marriage. Its analogies are erotic, yet pure, something our culture has struggled with reconciling. Parts of it may make you blush. They certainly made me blush writing about them. But remember, sex between a husband and wife is nothing to be ashamed of or embarrassed by, but celebrated as a gift from God. When you and your husband experience the passion God intended, I believe he stands up and cheers!

For too long the church has treated sex as a taboo subject. In the past, the extent of the church's teaching on sex has basically been, "If you're not married, don't do it. If you are married, don't talk about it." But the Bible talks about it, so we shouldn't be afraid to. As one pastor wrote, "If anyone says that sex is bad or dirty in itself, we have the entire Bible to contradict him."[9] Scripture shows us that sex is not an evil that marriage permits but a gift that marriage protects.

This positive perspective on sex and marriage is made clear even in the book title—some translations call it The Song of Songs, which literally means "The Greatest of All Songs."[10] It is similar to the titles "King of kings and Lord of lords" in the New Testament (Revelation 19:16) and "the Holy of Holies" in the Old Testament (Exodus 26:33 NASB). The superlative shows just how important the author considered romantic love between a man and woman to be—here we find The Greatest of All Songs.

Another unique feature is that this is truly the woman's song. The Shulammite woman is the main character, and the story is told from her point of view. We're privy to her private thoughts, her dreams, her longings—her own words. I think that's why we women can glean so much from her story. She is a woman like us, who speaks to us.

A woman being the principle character in a love song was very unusual during that time in history when women were treated like property. You'll see that God created her to be passionate and provocative—a powerful force in her own right.

I know for some of us a book about how to experience marital intimacy for a lifetime can be very painful. Perhaps you've made mistakes and haven't followed God's plan in the past. Maybe you believed the culture's view of sex and have the scars to prove it. It could be that you've thought about sex too much or too little. I want to promise you this: there's a lot of redemption in the Song of Solomon. There's a lot of redemption in Jesus—that's what the Bible is really all about. We walk. We fall. God picks us back up again and cheers for us to move forward in grace.

> Scripture shows us that sex is not an evil that marriage permits but a gift that marriage protects.

And so, let's walk together as we explore this jewel of a book filled with beautiful and powerful imagery. I think you'll agree that it's the most intimate, personal, and sensual book in all the Scriptures. In some ways it's an instruction manual for the mysteriously wondrous gift of sex; in other ways it's a treasure map for discovering jewels hidden deep within you. Some of the language seems to be written in code, so we'll need to decipher the hidden messages. It's going to be fun, and I can promise you'll never look at pomegranates and palm trees the same way again.

No matter what your experience with romance has been in the past, God has something special in store for you. Let's slip on our sandals with the Song's leading lady and join her on a journey of romance, marriage, and sexual intimacy that makes God's heart sing. Let's dust off the ancient words to uncover God's original design. I'm so glad we're doing this together.

Chapter 1

The Mystery of Physical Attraction

Until I was in the second grade, I was the tomboy of all tomboys. I could make skid marks in the street with my pink banana bike just as well as any old boy in the neighborhood. I threw rocks, climbed trees, and hiked through the drainage ditch that ran along the border of my backyard. My mother had a dickens of a time making me wear a shirt in the summer.

"Sharon Ann," she'd yell out the door as I sat perched in a tree. "Put on a shirt this minute!"

"Why?" I'd protest, "Stewart doesn't have to wear one!"

My brother was five years older, and he traipsed around the neighborhood bare-chested. Honestly, he didn't look any different from me, so why did I have to wear a shirt? I was pretty sure I'd gotten the short end of the stick being a girl.

But something happened in between the third and fifth grade. I think it had something to do with Isaac Thorpe's big blue eyes. He made me feel funny inside. I liked writing his name in my notebook. When he gave me a store-bought card on Valentine's Day, I thought it was the best day of my life. I decided I wanted to be a girl after all. I still liked hanging out with the boys—but for a whole different reason.

When we open the Song of Solomon, we meet a young girl who had newly discovered the thrill of a budding romance. She might have hung out with her brothers in the field all her life, but at some point, she decided she was glad she was a girl. The owner of the land her family leased made her feel funny inside. It was better than a Valentine card. She was lovestruck.

> Let him kiss me with the kisses of his mouth!
> For your love is better than wine;
>   your anointing oils are fragrant;
> your name is oil poured out;
>   therefore virgins love you.
> Draw me after you; let us run.
>   The king has brought me into his chambers.
>   (Song 1:2–4 ESV)

The Song of Solomon begins with a bang. Fireworks, to say the least! The Shulammite makes no bones about it: she wants her man and she wants him now. Right from the beginning, we meet a woman who is passionately in love and attracted to this man who has captured her—heart, mind, body, and soul. The story of this love song begins not at the moment the Shulammite caught Solomon's eye but at the time she was already head over heels in love.

Chances are you're already beyond the initial attraction and unrequited longings of the dating stage with your man. Perhaps, like the Shulammite, you've already flirted, teased, and snagged your hunky husband. So what's in these first two chapters about initial attraction for us? I'm glad you asked. One of the keys to lifelong intimacy is never letting the romancing end. When we stop flirting, the passion starts floundering. Marriage can subconsciously slide into the monotonous ho-hum of the mundane, leaving us wondering what happened to the love we felt in the early years. There's a lot of verbal foreplay and blantant flirting going on in the first two chapters of the Song. And here's what we'll see: the intentional teasing and enticing tempting don't stop. The unmarried Solomon and the Shulammite flirt with each other just as much in the beginning of their romance as they do at the end.

So let's see what the couple did, and most likely what we did, in the wooing stage so that we will still be wowing our men when we're old and gray.

The beginning of a romantic relationship is such an exciting, heady time. It starts with that initial attraction, the breathless wondering about the other person's feelings and the early stages of desire—all natural parts of the process as we walk toward commitment and deeper intimacy. We see all of this in the first chapters of the Song of Solomon, just as we see it in our own love stories.

It's a universal experience to be drawn to a specific person because of a certain something you can't quite put your finger on. Isn't it interesting that one woman will find a man attractive and another will not? Or that one man will find a woman alluring and another will not? Beauty (or handsomeness) truly is in the eye of the beholder. During my dating days, I was never attracted to the neat and tidy guys. Some of my friends swooned over guys with perfect hair who wore name-brand shirts and khaki pants. Not me. I was attracted to rugged guys with a bit of grit, dressed in jeans and a flannel shirt. Some are attracted to blue eyes, others to brown. Some to slim, others to stocky. Some to blondes, others to brunettes. Just the idea that men and women are drawn to varied physical traits shows the glorious creativity of God and the complexity of the human mind that we'll never fully understand.

> When we stop flirting, the passion starts floundering.

As we mature, we learn to look beyond the window dressing and into the heart—or at least we should. It takes time to discover what lies beneath the surface of a handsome exterior. But there is always that mysterious physical attraction that catches the eye.

So back to the *why*. Why is there the attraction between the opposite sexes? Whether it's Isaac Thorpe in the third grade or Steve Jaynes in my college Bible study, the answer is the same. God put it there. God fashioned man and woman to be attracted to one another, and that attraction extends to all our senses—what we taste, smell, hear, touch, see, and what we perceive lies beneath the physical appearance.

Kiss Me, and Kiss Me Again!

Did you notice how the Shulammite begins with a rush of longing? "Let him kiss me with the kisses of his mouth!" (1:2 ESV). Or, as another translation says, "Kiss me and kiss me again" (NLT). This is a verse your husband might want you to memorize in several different translations of the Bible. He'd be tickled if you memorized it in just one.

There's no warm-up as the book begins. No explanation. Plenty of desire. "For your love is better than wine" (v. 2 ESV). Right from the beginning we read of a woman who is amorously wistful and physically longing for intimacy. She wants him! She's hungry for his embrace! She's thirsty for his love! She wants him to kiss her and kiss her again! Remember when you felt that way?

One commentator wrote this about the suddenness of the Song's opening scene: "The style, simplicity, and insight of the first picture is a work of art. Not simply because it presents inner thoughts of a young princess, but because in doing so, it captures feelings that are universal at the birth of love and the suddenness with which they appear."[1]

C. S. Lewis described a similar passion in his book *The Four Loves*: "In one high bound [love] has overleaped the massive wall of our selfhood; it has made appetite itself altruistic, tossed personal happiness aside as a triviality and planted the interests of another in the centre of our being."[2] In her opening words the maiden takes "one high bound" into love.

Isn't that the way of love? Even if a man and woman have been friends for many years, there's a certain point when they realize they don't want to live without the other. Like falling asleep, falling in love can be gradual, and then all of a sudden.

The Shulammite longs for her lover's kisses and wants him to take her away where they can be alone. She refers to kissing his mouth, not just his lips. This is not just a peck she's talking about, but a passionately deep, hungry kiss—kisses that are more deliciously intoxicating than wine. One commentator wrote: "Touch and taste combine with the sound of the words as they roll off the tongue. The kisses on the mouth, the lovemaking, and the wine join together to provide readers with an introductory verse that plunges them into the heady waters of this poem. Here is no gradual acclimation, a step at a time, but rather a baptism by fire!"[3]

Have you ever wondered where the idea of kissing came from? When you think about it, it's rather strange. Try to describe a kiss to someone. Hmm. Just to hear about it doesn't sound all that exciting. Two faces pressed against each other. An exchange of spit. Tongues touching. It seems a bit awkward and messy. But to experience it is quite another story. Trying to describe a kiss is like trying to describe a magenta-streaked sunset to a blind person. Some things you just have to experience to comprehend the beauty.

A kiss can be the beginning or the end of a potential relationship. A kiss can prompt a desire to develop a romance further, or it can be a warning sign to run the other way. Scientists have begun to unravel the mystery of what actually happens in the human brain to cause one of these two reactions. Research scientist Sheril Kirshenbaum, author of *The Science of Kissing* noted:

> While we don't often think of them in this way, human lips are the body's most exposed erogenous zone. Packed with sensitive nerve endings, even a light brush sends a cascade of information to our brains helping us to decide whether we want to continue and what might happen next.
>
> Lip contact involves five of our 12 cranial nerves as we engage all of our senses to learn more about a partner. Electric impulses bounce between the brain, lips, tongue and skin, which can lead to the feeling of being on a natural "high" because of a potent cocktail of chemical messengers involved.
>
> A passionate kiss acts like a drug, causing us to crave the other person thanks to a neurotransmitter called dopamine. This is the same substance involved in taking illegal substances such as cocaine, which is why the novelty of a new romance can feel so addictive. Dopamine is involved in sensations of reward, making us feel intense desire that can lead to feelings of euphoria, insomnia, and loss of appetite, and it is only one actor in the great chemical ballet happening in our bodies.
>
> And then there are physical changes. A kiss can cause our blood vessels to dilate, our pulse to quicken and cheeks to flush. . . . In other words, the body's response mirrors many of the same symptoms frequently associated with falling in love.[4]

I hope I haven't just ruined kissing for you. Here's what I want us to see: kissing is so much more than two people locking lips. Think of all the intricacies God put into crafting what happens in the human body with that one simple act. Studies now show that even a man's testosterone (which causes his sex drive) is transferred to the woman via his salvia. When you think about it, there's nothing simple about a simple kiss. Author Emil Ludwig wrote, "The decision to kiss for the first time is the most crucial in any love story. It changes the relationship of two people much more strongly than even the final surrender; because this kiss already has within it that surrender."[5]

Do you remember the first time you and your husband kissed? I can remember it like it was yesterday. It was one of those good-night kisses by the door at the end of a date. An awkward pause . . . then the lean. Slow motion. Oh my! After that kiss, I walked into my apartment, closed the door, and leaned back with a sigh. It was the beginning of many kisses to come. As the dancer Agnes de Mille said, "Then I did the simplest thing in the world. I leaned down . . . and kissed him. And the world cracked open."[6]

I met Steve Jaynes at a college Bible study. I walked into my friend's apartment, and there he was. Sitting on the worn carpet wearing scruffy jeans and a red flannel shirt rolled halfway up his muscular forearms. His back was leaning against the stark wall with legs outstretched and crossed at the ankles. His angular face needed a shave, and a chipped front tooth added to his brawn. His strong jawline said *brave*. An open Bible said *character*. His easy laugh said *joy*. Then he looked up at me, and my heart melted in the chocolate pool of his eyes.

That sounds so gushy gooey! But, girls, that's how it happened. The moment I laid eyes on Steve Jaynes something leapt in my heart. I was smitten. If it wasn't love at first sight, it was something close. Thankfully, it was mutual.

I know it's not always like that when couples meet. I daresay some of the most successful marriages are the ones where the couples started out as friends and then grew into romantic love. With Steve and me, though, it was more like, *Boom!* Right away I thought, *Who is that guy? Where has he been all my life?* "All my life" being a mere twenty-three years.

I'll admit, Steve and I kissed a lot during our brief dating days. All five of those cranial nerves were fired up and ready to go. The closer we got to the wedding day, the more we kissed. It was ridiculous, but we didn't think so.

Just the other day I asked Steve, "What do you miss about the dating days?"

He replied, "I'm not sure, but I know what you're going to say. Kissing!"

He was right. Don't get me wrong. We still kiss. But I miss long-kissing for kissing's sake that's not leading anywhere.

Interestingly, the Greek word for worship, *proskyneo,* comes from two words: *pros*, meaning "toward," and *kyneo*, meaning "to kiss." While we do not worship our husbands, even our kisses can be an act of worship and adoration of God for the man he has given us.

Now for the *why* of the kiss. God wired you to enjoy kissing your man, even to yearn for it. He fashioned all those nerve impulses, hungry hormones, blood vessel dilations, and chemical reactions for a specific reason: mutual attraction and enjoyment. Isn't he ingenious? And you thought it was just a kiss. The next time you kiss your husband, think about how happy the Father is that you're enjoying something he created just for you. You might even want to commit to kissing your husband at least once a day—even when you're angry or frustrated. (Don't give me that look.)

The Sensuality of Scent

Since God created the first rose garden and gardenia bush, men and women have been attracted to various scents. The fragrance industry grew to a worth of $38.8 billion in 2018,[7] and there's no slowing down. One thing we learn about attraction in the Song of Solomon is that it involves a variety of senses. In the first verse the Shulammite engages the sense of touch and taste. In the second she brings in the sense of smell.

Okay, let's go ahead and say it, she was *turned on* by the way he smelled. Had she lived today, she might have said, "He's lookin' good and smellin' good."

> Pleasing is the fragrance of your perfumes;
> your name is like perfume poured out. (v. 3)

Remember, back in their day men and women didn't bathe very often. They often wore perfumed ointment and olive-based oils to protect their skin from the arid climate of the Middle East and to mask the smell of their unwashed bodies.

I was surprised to learn that men and women are attracted to each other's natural scents. I'm not talking about cologne or perfume, but just regular unhampered and not-tampered-with scent. An article in *Psychology Today* revealed the following:

> Everyone knows what it's like to be powerfully affected by a partner's smell—witness men who bury their noses in their wives' hair and women who can't stop sniffing their boyfriends' T-shirts. And couples have long testified to the ways scent-based chemistry affects their relationships. . . .
>
> Sexual attraction remains one of life's biggest mysteries. . . . Some researchers think scent could be the hidden cosmological constant in the sexual universe, the missing factor that explains who we end up with. It may even explain why we feel "chemistry"—or "sparks" or "electricity"—with one person and not with another.
>
> Physical attraction itself may literally be based on smell. We discount the importance of scent-centric communication only because it operates on such a subtle level. . . . As a result, we may

> find ourselves drawn to the counter attendant at the local drugstore, but have no idea why—or, conversely, find ourselves put off by potential dating partners even though they seem perfect on paper.[8]

I would have never guessed that men and women were attracted to each other because of the way they smelled. Here's our takeaway: God put the attraction to a person's scent in us, and we don't even realize it's there or that it's happening. Again, we can see the intentionality of our fascinating Creator to fashion even our sense of smell for mutual attraction that leads to romance.

The Shulammite was no doubt bedazzled by Solomon's handsome face, but she was also intoxicated with his yummy smell. I can picture her wanting to nuzzle her nose in the crook of his neck and breathe in the scent of him.

Do you remember wearing a certain body lotion or perfume that your husband loved when you were dating? Do you remember a certain scent about him? It could be something as simple as the deodorant he wore. Since you're already going to kiss your husband once a day, why not lean in and inhale his scent? Then tell him he smells good enough to eat. Just a thought.

The Allure of Character

The Shulammite was drawn to more than Solomon's intoxicating perfumed oil or the scent of his skin; she said that *his name* was "like perfume poured out" (v. 3). Just the mention of his name made her woozy with love.

In Solomon's day a person's name had meaning. A name told you something about the person's character or physical appearance. The name *Esau* means "hairy," and the Esau we see in Genesis was indeed hairy. *Jacob* means "trickster," which fit the biblical Jacob perfectly. *Moses* means "drawn out of water," and he was. *Solomon* means "peace," and that was what he brought to Israel. The Shulammite said that her lover's name was "like perfume poured out"—an image that often referred to offerings poured out to God in the temple. So we can surmise, then, that her lover was a godly man. Beyond his physical appearance, the Shulammite was attracted to his spiritual character and public reputation. Solomon would later write in the book of Ecclesiastes, "A good reputation is more valuable than costly perfume" (7:1 NLT).

The NASB translates Song 1:3, "Your name is like purified oil." Purified oil was extra-virgin olive oil, the purest form from the first pressing. Back in their day this oil was so special that it was only used in the temple for the lampstand that burned night and day. In addition to being the best oil, it was the best of the best given to God.[9] So in a way she was saying that Solomon's character was the best of the best. Can you imagine how your husband would feel if you told him, "You're not just the best; you're the best of the best"?

She concludes the section with this thought: "No wonder the young women love you!" (v. 3).

Physical attraction may be the catalyst to entertaining a possible relationship, but it is not enough to sustain it. The popular reality television shows *The Bachelor* and *The Bachelorette* have proven this time and time again. Men and women are attracted to each other and make microwave decisions based on physical appearance, "chemistry," and "connectedness," only to become dismayed when the cameras stop rolling and real life slaps them in the face. This is not to say that physical attraction is bad, not by a long shot. You should never marry someone that you are not physically attracted to. The point is, you can hide poor character under makeup, stylish clothes, and exotic dates for a while, but eventually that character will creep through the cracks and sully the pretty window dressing.

It is often only when the bachelor or bachelorette sees the prerecorded footage—the actions he or she was not aware of during the process—that the poor character hidden beneath the attractive exterior becomes apparent. Here's the truth we must remember: it is the inner qualities that last long after the skin sags, the hair thins, the waist widens, and the wrinkles ripple the once-smooth surface. For two lives to be truly intertwined for a lifetime, love must look beyond the outward appearance to the soul.

As I've often heard, character is who you are when no one is looking. To the Shulammite, Solomon was much more than a handsome face. He was a man of character who was the same whether he was near her or far away. She might have been beguiled by his handsome appearance, but she was captivated by his holy character.

> Physical attraction may be the catalyst to entertaining a possible relationship, but it is not enough to sustain it.

I have to stop here and address the elephant in the room. You might be thinking, *Isn't this the same guy who had seven hundred wives and three hundred concubines?* Most likely it is. Some believe that Song was written early in Solomon's reign, before all that took place. The Shulammite mentions his youthful exuberance like a gazelle and his well-sculpted features like chiseled stone. Most likely she was his first love.

Solomon started out being known as a man of great wisdom, but in his later years his success turned his heart away from God and toward foreign women and their gods (1 Kings 11:4). God had instructed Solomon not to make treaties with other nations, but he did. With each treaty, he acquired a new wife from that nation. Even though his collection of women was more of a political move than a romantic one, it still eventually led his heart away from God. Perhaps that is why one of his later books, Ecclesiastes, is one of the saddest in the entire Bible.

I wish we could pretend that Solomon's downfall didn't happen.

Here's what we can remember: Solomon started out well. He was considered the wisest man on earth at the time. However, even the wisest among us can deviate from the truth if they allow themselves to veer from God's plan and think more highly of themselves than they ought.

The Song of Solomon clearly portrays monogamous love between one man and one woman for a lifetime. That's what God really wants us to see. Sex was his idea, and he wants husbands and wives to experience it without regret.

Who Is That Hot Babe?

Now that we know what the Shulammite thought about Solomon, how did Solomon feel about her? When I met Steve I certainly wondered how he felt about me. *Does he think I'm pretty? Could a guy like him ever be attracted to a girl like me? Would he like to kiss me?* While the Shulammite was wildly attracted to Solomon, she doubted he could be attracted to a girl like her. She was so insecure about her appearance, she wondered why any man would give her a second glance. Listen to how she described herself:

> How right they are to adore you!
> Dark am I, yet lovely,
>   daughters of Jerusalem,
> dark like the tents of Kedar,
>   like the tent curtains of Solomon.
> Do not stare at me because I am dark,
>   because I am darkened by the sun.
> My mother's sons were angry with me
>   and made me take care of the vineyards;
>   my own vineyard I had to neglect. (Song 1:4–6)

"I'm just a lowly field hand with sunburned ruddy skin," she said. "Don't even look at me. I'm so ashamed of my appearance."

The Shulammite was a hardworking farm girl who labored away in her stepbrothers' vineyards. Most likely her father was deceased and her mom had remarried, as she referred to the field hands as "her mother's sons." This conjures up the picture of Cinderella with her evil stepsisters, but with angry stepbrothers instead. In all probability the brothers leased the land from King Solomon, which would explain why he was perusing the vineyard when he first noticed her.

We don't know why her stepbrothers were angry with her. It could be that they were jealous that the king paid attention to her, or because she was their mom's favorite. We do know she felt animosity from them. And then came along Cinderella's handsome prince, only in this version of the story, he was a king.

The Shulammite bemoaned the fact that she had been so busy looking out for her brothers' interests that she hadn't had time to take care of her own vineyard, her personal appearance. The girl had lived a hard life. In the poem she interwove the glaring heat of the sun, the burning anger of her brothers, and the searing stares of other women. She knew rejection, shame, and abuse by name. She compared her appearance to the tents of Kedar, which were tents made of dark or black wool by a Bedouin tribe. She also compared her skin to the dark purple curtains in Solomon's temple. Both of these comparisons point to sunburned skin that was ruddy and rough.

The Shulammite's self-worth was as flimsy as the tent flaps blowing in the arid wind. You can tell how self-conscious she was when she told the women not to stare at her. At the same time, she knew there was something about her that was lovely.

Historians have explained, "In the ancient world, fair skin was preferred to dark skin for class reasons (rather than racial reasons)."[10] Vast numbers of people were farmers, and skin darkened by the sun meant they were commoners. The aristocracy had fairer skin due to their lack of time in the sun—they were indoor girls. Fair skin was considered exotic.

When I first read the Shulammite's words, I thought, *I'm just like her*. No, I'm not weathered from working in the fields, but I am insecure about my appearance. And to be honest I haven't met many women who aren't. There's always something we're not satisfied with. Booty too big, breasts too small. Waistline too thick, hair too thin. Lashes too short, nose too long. Skin too dark, skin too pale. On and on we go.

Rather than:

> Mirror, mirror, on the wall,
> Who's the fairest of them all?

We're more inclined to say:

> Mirror, mirror, on the wall,
> Sometimes I don't like you, not at all.

We compare ourselves with airbrushed models and hold up a culturally defined standard of beauty that is unattainable. Those models don't actually look like the magazine images they appear in, yet we feel "less than" because we don't look like people who aren't even real. Have mercy! Advertisers thrive on making women feel insecure about their appearance to sell their products . . . and it works. But no matter how many procedures they've had, products they've used, or provocative styles they've tried, women still can't shake their body image struggles.

It's difficult for a woman to give herself freely and completely to her husband if she feels inhibited by insecurity. She will hold back and try to hide what she considers unattractive under the sheets. You know what the Shulammite has taught me about this? I need to focus less on what I see in the mirror and more on the love I'd see when I look in my husband's eyes.

Beauty comes in all shapes, sizes, and colors. What did Solomon think of the Shulammite's appearance? He found her alluringly beautiful. I imagine when he first laid eyes on her, his world began to spin in slow motion—taking in her every move. Listen to these lovestruck words:

> I liken you, my darling, to a mare
> among Pharaoh's chariot horses.
> Your cheeks are beautiful with earrings,
> your neck with strings of jewels.
> We will make you earrings of gold,
> studded with silver. (vv. 9–11)

I don't know about you, but I wouldn't be too thrilled if my husband told me I looked like a horse. In Solomon's culture, however, it was quite a compliment. The king only used the most beautiful horses to pull his chariots, mostly white Arabian horses. In ancient artwork these horses were often depicted with bejeweled bridles and headgear. They would certainly stand out in a crowd of the typical brown-and-black variety. It was as if Solomon were saying, "You stand out in the crowd. I can spot you from a mile away. You're eye-catchingly beautiful and breathtakingly magnificent."

After the second millennium the royals only used stallions because the female mares were too distracting. And, believe me, this man was distracted. Solomon poured out positive affirmation about the Shulammite's appearance and washed away her insecurities.

This reminds me of one of my father-in-law's stories about when he was away at war in the Aleutian Islands.

"I wrote Mary Ellen and asked her to send me a picture of her legs," he said with a chuckle.

"Did she send you one?" I asked.

"She sure did," he replied.

"What ever happened to the picture, Dad?"

He pulled out his wallet and showed it to me. He was eighty-two years old at the time, so this picture had been in his wallet for sixty-two years. No doubt he thought his bride's legs were as beautiful as the mares' legs were among Pharaoh's chariots.

I'm not sure what you thought of your appearance when you first caught your husband's eye, but, girl, he thought you were beautiful.

Things Were Heating Up

It may seem a bit odd that the Song jumps from Solomon telling the Shulammite how beautiful she is to her daydreaming about the day when they can finally make love as husband and wife. But, then again, maybe not. Words of admiration can make a woman feel a bit woozy, especially when they're from the man she loves.

> While the king was at his table,
> my perfume spread its fragrance.
> My beloved is to me a sachet of myrrh
> resting between my breasts.
> My beloved is to me a cluster of henna blossoms
> from the vineyards of En Gedi. (vv. 12–14)

The ESV translates verse 12 closer to its literal meaning: "The king was on his *couch*, my nard gave forth its fragrance" (emphasis added). Solomon and the Shulammite weren't lying on his couch together, but she was certainly dreaming about it. She imagined her perfume releasing its scent as her skin warmed to his touch.

In Solomon's day women who could afford it wore a small leather pouch filled with perfume such as myrrh around their necks. Myrrh is a resin from a thorny, ragged-looking balsam tree, something like an acacia, which grows in Arabia, Ethiopia, and India. It was commonly used as an alluring female perfume. It was also used to perfume royal nuptial robes, perhaps preparing the couple for what came after the "I dos" (Psalm 45:8). Sometimes women would sleep with the perfume box tucked between their breasts. Then, in the morning, they would carry the scent with them throughout the day. The Shulammite dreamed about the day when Solomon would be like that sachet of myrrh, resting between her breasts.

This is going to be important a little later in the Song, when—spoiler alert!—that dream becomes a reality.

When you were dating your husband, did you ever dream about the day you would finally come together sexually? A time when you would live together as Mr. and Mrs.? I bet you did.

I remember the week before my wedding day, I drove ninety miles from my hometown to Chapel Hill, North Carolina, just to sit in the apartment Steve and I would share as husband and wife. The furniture was in place, the curtains were hung, and the pillows were fluffed, all waiting for our arrival. I opened the windows and lay across the bed to peer out at the neighborhood and daydream. I imagined my new life with Steve, which would begin in seven days. I think that's what the Shulammite was doing. She'd opened the windows and was enjoying the gentle breeze, imagining a day when she could be united to her man in every way.

I'm so glad that the Shulammite has reminded me of the longing I had more than thirty-five years ago, so that I can appreciate what I have today. I hope she has reminded you too.

The Divine Design of a Creative God

Attraction between men and women is such a beautifully intricate part of God's design. As we learn more about the ways our very bodies have been engineered to respond to stimuli like kissing, smelling, and touching, we start to see just what a creative and ingenious God we serve. In fact we can see even in the opening passage of the Bible how he had planned from the very beginning for the power of attraction.

Genesis, the first book of the Bible, begins with God speaking the world into existence. He decorated the sky with the sun, moon, and stars, and scattered seed of every kind in the soil. He released flocks of birds into the sky, swarms of insects into the air, and schools of fish into the sea. On the fifth day, God created all the creeping animals (1:1–25). As the sun set on the first five days of creation, he looked at what he had made and "saw that it was good" (v. 25).

Then, when he created man, God did something different from simply speaking. The Creator bent low, took a holy handful of dust in his palms, and formed an image bearer to reflect his likeness: Adam. Afterward he said, "It is *not* good for the man to be alone" (2:18, emphasis added). That's where you and I come in.

"For Adam no suitable helper was found. So the Lord God caused the man to fall into a deep sleep; and while he was sleeping, he took one of the man's ribs and then closed up the place with flesh. Then the Lord God made a woman from the rib he had taken out of man, and he brought her to the man" (vv. 20–22).

The NASB says God "fashioned" Eve (v. 22). He took extra special care when he created her. As a matter of fact, she was God's grand finale! Up to this point in the Genesis recording of creation, Adam had remained silent. However, when he laid eyes on the fair Eve, I imagine he said, "Whoa! Now this is good!" We don't know for sure, but we do know that his first recorded words after seeing God's magnificent gift to him were, "This is now bone of my bones and flesh of my flesh; she shall be called 'woman,' for she was taken out of man" (v. 23).

Adam's name for this new creature, *woman*, essentially means "out of me" or "mine." Eve was the reason for man's first poetry and the object of his greatest joy.

Eve was created to complete man like two pieces of a puzzle fitting together. The word *complete* means "to fill up; that which is required to supply a deficiency; one of two mutually completing parts." God placed an extra dose of testosterone in Adam and a greater supply of estrogen in Eve. When Adam's testosterone laid eyes on Eve's estrogen, the attraction was like the positive and negative poles of a magnet coming together. *Boom!*

Adam was enamored with Eve's body, her eyes, her hair, her voice, and her scent. Why? Because that's the way God planned it. In Genesis 2 we see God's original plan for man and woman: "Adam and his wife were both naked, and they felt no shame" (v. 25). They had nothing to fear and nothing to hide. God gave them the gift of sex. "Be fruitful and multiply," he instructed them (1:28 ESV). Enjoy!

> Eve was the reason for man's first poetry and the object of his greatest joy.

Notice that, while God told Adam and Eve to be fruitful and multiply, there is no mention of children or procreation in the Song of Songs. This is truly a celebration of romantic love, marital commitment, and sexual intimacy, and we're just getting started.

So where did the physical attraction and desire come from? God put it there! It was his gift to them. It is God's gift to us. But I'm running a bit ahead of myself. We're going to talk about the gift of sex in chapter 4. For now let's just rejoice in knowing that the attraction between a man and a woman was designed by God, for our pleasure and for his glory.

Chapter 2

The Deepening of Desire

Steve and I had scheduled a date for dinner and a movie, which was quite a splurge for two single college students pooling pennies. But I really wasn't all that interested in the dinner or the movie. What I was interested in was getting to know more about the man taking me out—what he liked and disliked, his aspirations and goals for the future, the depth of his relationship with God. I also looked forward to the good-night kiss. Okay, let's call it what it was: the *looooong* kisses. The kind that would have had my mom blinking the porch light had I been living at home. I bet you dreamed about it too.

The more I got to know this man mentally, emotionally, and spiritually, the deeper my desire grew to know him physically. But I also knew that developing an intimate friendship is the foundation for maintaining a forever relationship. Deep, abiding friendship is a cornerstone for a marriage that goes the distance.

Steve and I both loved Jesus and dancing. You don't see those two "loves" in the same sentence often, and I knew I had hit the jackpot. We also enjoyed reading books that caused us to pause and ponder, developing lasting relationships with friends, and playing card games with other couples. As a bonus we both were working on dovetailing college degrees that would lead to a future common profession. We knew very early that we were going to be forever friends. Solomon saw that same potential in the Shulammite.

Twice in Songs 1, Solomon called the Shulammite his "darling" (vv. 9, 15). The Hebrew word *rayah* is the female form of a noun that means "companion" and is translated "darling" in the NIV, "dearest" in the NEB, and "love" in the NRSV.[1] It is like the French *petite amie*, which carries the meaning of "sweetheart" and is literally "little friend" in English.[2] The Shulammite was not only Solomon's lover but also his intimate friend and would become his lifelong companion.

> Developing an intimate friendship is the foundation for maintaining a forever relationship.

What comes to mind when you hear the word *intimate*? In the movie *Same Kind of Different as Me*, the lead couple had a heated argument.

"We haven't been intimate in two years!" the husband yelled.

"No, we haven't slept together in two years! We haven't been intimate in ten years!" the wife yelled back.[3]

Obviously they saw the word *intimate* from very different perspectives.

So what does "being intimate" entail? Certainly there's physical intimacy. But true intimacy involves much more than a physical union. It is the intertwining of two hearts through mutual sharing and passing years.

Sheldon Vanauken wrote about his love with his wife, Davy, in the book *A Severe Mercy*. In a poignant paragraph he said:

> What is it that draws two people into closeness and love? Of course there's the mystery of physical attraction, but beyond that it's the things they share. We both love strawberries and ships and collies and poems and all beauty, and all those things bind us together. Those sharings just happened to be; but what we must do now is share *everything*. Everything! If one of us likes *anything*, there must be something to like in it—and the other one must find it. Every

> single thing that either of us likes. That way we shall create a thousand strands, great and small, that will link us together. Then we shall be so close that it would be impossible—unthinkable—for either of us to suppose that we could ever recreate such closeness with anyone else. And our trust in each other will not only be based on love and loyalty, but on the *fact* of a thousand sharings—a thousand strands twisted into something unbreakable.[4]

Unbreakable. I like that word, especially when applied to marriage. Sheldon and Davy called this resolve the "Shining Barrier," the shield of their love. They considered it "a walled garden. A fence around a young tree to keep the deer from nibbling it. A fortified place with the walls and watchtowers gleaming white like the cliffs of England."[5]

Just like Sheldon and Davy, and Solomon and the Shulammite, we need to find ways to protect our friendship above all others. A wise couple considers ways to keep the friendship going and growing. It is often after a married couple has experienced a fun time as friends that they experience the most passionate romance as lovers.

Did you notice in chapter 1 that the Shulammite has a sudden interest in sheep?

> Tell me, you whom I love,
> where you graze your flock
> and where you rest your sheep at midday. (v. 7)

She wanted to be near her man and showed interest in what interested him—sheep. When I met Steve, I took a serious interest in college intramural basketball. Honestly, I couldn't have cared less about the game. What I was interested in was number 3. The way his arms arced and muscles flexed when he took that three-point shot. The way he acted as if he didn't notice that I was watching his every move. Yep. I loved me some intramural basketball.

I bet you and your husband took on some new interests when you were dating. He probably even loved the mall! A smart couple will continue sharing commonalities throughout their marriage. True, your husband most likely won't jump at the chance to carry your shopping bags your whole married life, and he'll probably understand if you don't enjoy watching him change the oil like you did when you were dating. But it is crucial to lifelong friendship to have shared activities that create an unbreakable bond. The Shulammite will later say about Solomon, "This is my beloved, this is my friend" (5:16). Their friendship started at the genesis of their relationship and continued till the end.

We're going to talk more about the importance of growing and maintaining intimate friendship in chapter 7. For now, know that while the couple was wildly attracted to each other, they were also developing a friendship that would last a lifetime.

The Elegant Dance of Mutual Praise

"I love you."

"I love you more."

"No, I love you more."

I wonder if you and your husband have ever bantered those words back and forth.

Just as important as the actions we take to develop a relationship are the words we speak to deepen it. At the end of chapter 1 and the beginning of chapter 2 of the Song, the couple volleys compliments back and forth at breakneck speed. Make no mistake, they are blatantly flirting. Solomon tells the Shulammite what he thinks about her. Then she quickly replies with what she thinks about him. Oh, friend, do you remember you and your husband trying to "outnice" each other during the dating days? Why in the world would you ever stop?

Remember, the Shulammite maiden was extremely insecure about her sun-scorched appearance. How precious that God provided a new mirror in which she could see her true beauty—the man who loved her. Let's eavesdrop on Solomon and his Shulammite as they ping-ponged their playful praise.

Solomon:

> How beautiful you are, my darling!
> Oh, how beautiful!
> Your eyes are doves. (1:15)

The Shulammite:

> How handsome you are, my beloved!
> Oh, how charming! (v. 16)

I love that he used the word *beautiful* twice when describing her. It's as if saying it once just didn't do her justice. Then she bantered back with a double dose as well: "How handsome you are, my beloved! Oh, how charming!" The words *beautiful* and *handsome* are actually the feminine and masculine form of the same Hebrew word, showing their mutual affection and passion for each other. Their words are what one commentator called, "an elegant dance of mutual praise."[6] Solomon led the dance by taking the first two steps forward, and she followed by taking two steps with him.

Solomon called her his *rayati*, the Hebrew word for "darling" or "my love." She in turn called him her *dodi*, the Hebrew word for "beloved." Steve and I have decided that these are our new pet names for each other. You might want to do that too!

One thing is for sure: they both knew right from the beginning that their feelings were mutual. This was no guessing game. If my husband has to wonder how I feel about him, I'm not doing my job very well. We learn from these lovers the importance of both parties making sure the other feels loved, adored, and preferred.

Still, she had trouble believing him, and she voiced her insecurity again in chapter 2.

> I am a rose of Sharon,
>   a lily of the valleys. (2:1)

At first glance we might think she was comparing herself to a beautiful flower, but it was far from it. The actual plants referred to as the "rose of Sharon" and "lily of the valleys" are bulb-type plants, lotus flowers, or common field flowers. We might think of it as her saying, "I'm just a dandelion in a field of weeds." In other words, "I'm so ordinary."

What woman hasn't felt that way? We look in the mirror and think, *Humph. I'm just a plain old girl, getting older by the day. Nothing special here.*

But notice how the Shulammite's suitor disagreed with her estimation of herself!

> Like a lily among thorns
>   is my darling among the young women. (v. 2)

"You're no ordinary flower at all!" he replied. "As a matter of fact, every other woman looks like a bramble bush of thorns compared with you!"

Solomon gave her the gift every woman longs for—the gift of being preferred. He complimented her in the one area in which she felt most insecure. I imagine her heart opened like a morning glory in the warmth of his words. Once again Solomon was saying to his Shulammite, "Let me be your mirror."

And what did the Shulammite say to him in return?

Like an apple tree among the trees of the forest
is my beloved among the young men.
I delight to sit in his shade,
and his fruit is sweet to my taste. (v. 3)

In other words, "If I'm no ordinary flower, then you're no ordinary tree. You're a fruit tree among all the other ordinary fruitless trees in the forest." Apple trees, or as some commentators translate the original word, apricot trees, were very rare in the Near East. So she let him know that he was rare among men—that he gave nourishment for her soul, shade from the scorching heat, and protection from the elements. His kisses were sweet, and his love was shade and security itself. She felt completely safe with him. He was everything she could have ever dreamed of. Paul wrote that a husband should nourish, protect, and cherish his wife (Ephesians 5:29 AMP). That is exactly what the Shulammite found in her man—and she let him know it.

In a growing relationship it's so important that a woman not only receive compliments but also give them. That's true when we're dating as well as when we're married. The giving and receiving of compliments shouldn't end until we hear the words "May he/she rest in peace." Did you know that your husband questions his manhood on a regular basis? Guys often feel a need to prove themselves in their work, in their play, and in their marriage. Watch guys at the gym (I mean that in the most innocent way), and you may notice how they compare themselves with each other. That is just a glimpse of how they compare themselves in other arenas of life. Men operate under the burden of performance that leads them to question their ability and impact constantly. From boyhood to manhood they hold themselves to a self-imposed measuring stick that rarely says they're enough.

I don't want my husband to have to go somewhere other than home to be affirmed. I bet you don't either. Let your husband know that, among all the ordinary trees in the forest, he is an apple tree that produces extraordinary fruit. Give *him* the gift of being preferred. Tell him often that you love tasting his delicious juicy fruit and sitting under the protective branches of his strong, hunky arms. I bet you'll see a yummy smile come on his face.

Solomon and the Shulammite almost seem like they were making a game out of giving compliments, or maybe they just couldn't contain their excitement. Either way, they were doing more than simply pouring out admiration; they were wooing with words. This makes me stop and think, *When was the last time I complimented my husband or let him know that I desired him physically? When was the last time I told him that his love was security and protection itself? That he is the handsomest, wisest, most exciting man alive? That I love kissing him? That I enjoy being near him?* I wonder, when was the last time you let your man know that, even though you've been married for quite some time, he's still everything you ever longed for?

> The giving and receiving of compliments shouldn't end until we hear the words "May he/she rest in peace."

Anne Lamott said, "A good marriage is where both people feel like they're getting the better end of the deal."[7] When I make my husband feel that I think I'm getting the better part of the deal, he feels like he is getting the better part of the deal. It's a win-win.

One of the most effective ways to grow and maintain intimacy happens way before we get between the sheets. It starts with what happens between the lips—the words that come out of our mouths. The Bible says that "death and life are in the power of the tongue" (Proverbs 18:21 ESV), and the death and life of a relationship are in the power of the tongue as well. Let's make sure our words are speaking life.

Growing Desire

My friend Shawna and I were having lunch, chatting about her bridal showers, wedding plans, and honeymoon destination. At one point her eyes teared up and she looked ten shades of nervous. "Sharon, I am having so much trouble waiting. When we're kissing, it's so hard to stop," she confided. "Do you know what I'm talking about?"

"Yes, I know what you're talking about. And it's nothing to be ashamed of. That's the way God planned it," I replied. "If you *weren't* anxious to have sex with your fiancé, then I'd be worried."

We both laughed, and the conversation took an easy turn toward the natural desire for physical intimacy and the joys of sex between a husband and wife. She left not feeling guilty about her physical urges but excited about what God had in store for both of them. That is the growing passion we see happening between the Shulammite and Solomon in this chapter. Their romance was heating up, and it was getting harder and harder to wait.

At this point in the couple's relationship, the beloved only praises his beloved's head and neck because that is all he can see. Sure, he can make out her shape beneath the working woman's robe, but he was doing what I recommend to dating folks all the time: keeping his attention above the neck. It's a pretty good rule of thumb in the dating phase of a relationship.

Don't let the phrase "our bed is verdant" (NIV) or "our couch is green" (ESV) in Song 1:16 throw you. Yes, the Hebrew word used here is translated "bed"; however, the couple had not *gone to* bed yet. We'll have proof of that later in the Song. Her mentioning that their bed was verdant is most likely a metaphor comparing their growing love to the shade of a spreading tree and the fruitfulness of the love that the couple enjoyed.[8] She saw their love as growing deep roots, spreading branches, and reaching to heights not yet known. I think she was also flirting with her man, perhaps pointing to a time when the bed metaphor would become a reality.

Just as she teasingly mentioned the bed, Solomon followed her tree analogy by referencing the beams of their future home, reflecting on the strength and stable support of their love canopy.

> The beams of our house are cedars;
> our rafters are firs. (Song 1:17)

They were *both* dreaming about the day when the bed would not be a metaphor of sexual intimacy but a reality. One thing is for sure: the Shulammite was lovestruck and lovesick for her man. She was just about to faint at the mere thought of him.

> Strengthen me with raisin cakes,
> refresh me with apples,
> for I am weak with love. (2:5 NLT)

She was what we might call weak in the knees over this guy. "Somebody help me," she could have cried. "Give me a glass of water (or raisins and apples will be fine)." In ancient times raisins and apples were considered the fruits of love, or aphrodisiacs; these are a couple more code words in the poem. No doubt her comparing Solomon to an apple tree stirred her desire to enjoy his fruit. She went on to imagine the day when he would touch her . . . every part of her.

> His left arm is under my head,
> and his right arm embraces me. (v. 6)

The ESV has a more literal translation: "His left hand is under my head, and his right *hand* embraces me!" (emphasis added). One expert explained, "The Hebrew word translated *embrace* usually means to embrace lovingly, to fondle or stimulate with gentle stroking."[9] She was picturing them lying side by side with his left arm under her head and his right hand caressing her or touching her body. Is this really in the Bible? Yep. She was dreaming of making love. As another commentator said, "Where in human literature does one find a text so erotic and yet so moral as this?"[10]

Romantic love stirs up sexual desire. That's nothing to be ashamed of. God planned it that way. However, sexual desire does not prove romantic love. Those stirrings can be just lust. That's *not* the way God planned it. A person can have sexual desire, or lust, without romantic love, but romantic love that does not stir up feelings of sexual desire is in trouble.

The Shulammite was naturally anxious for the day she could be with her man in every way, but she also knew the importance of waiting for the right time, of setting good boundaries to contain the kindling of romance before it burst into flames.

You might wonder how I know she's simply dreaming about being physically intimate rather than actually engaging in foreplay. The next verse tells us.

> Daughters of Jerusalem, I charge you
> by the gazelles and by the does of the field:
> Do not arouse or awaken love
> until it so desires. (v. 7)

This was a splash of water on the Shulammite's steamy imaginings. She was reminding her friends (and herself) about the importance of timing, and we'll see the same reminder come up two other times later in the Song (5:8; 8:4). Many men and women bring sexual baggage into a marriage—suitcases of regret that open up in the heat of passion and litter the marriage bed with images time can't erase. The Shulammite resolved not to pack that bag but to wait until the time was right. I think she was also reminding herself.

Levi Lusko, in his book *Swipe Right*, wrote, "Unfortunately when you take a bite from what God has told you not to eat, it can keep you from experiencing what he wants you to have (Genesis 2:17)."[11] That's what the Shulammite was reminding her friends and herself. Sex outside of marriage is in the Bible plenty of times, but never with a good outcome. It's not that God is a spoilsport. Quite the contrary. God created sex. God wants men and women to have the best sex possible—lifelong intimacy at its best—and he knows that only happens within the boundaries of marriage between a husband and wife. He created sex to be not only pleasurable but also powerful. That's why he put rules in place—not to take away joy but to add to it. So we have to remember what Lusko said succinctly: "*Now* yells louder, but *later* lasts longer."[12]

Besides, there's more to the journey to the kind of relational intimacy God wants us to experience than just jumping straight to sex. There is an aspect of discovery at play, as we spend time together, grow closer spiritually and emotionally, and learn each other's true character. While it takes only a few minutes to decide if we like the package, it takes more time to lift the lid and explore the heart.

The reality today, though, is that 80 percent of evangelical Christians do not wait until marriage to have sex.[13] So chances are the majority of women reading this book were not virgins when they got married and may be feeling regret, shame, guilt, or self-condemnation. But here's what you need to know. Our God is a God of redemption. That means he takes the messed-up parts of our lives, turns them around, cleans them up, and makes them into something good. He is a God of new beginnings. I've often heard it said that we cannot go back and make a new start, but we can start now and make a new ending. No matter what you've done in your past, you can begin again with a new present that leads to a fabulous future.

God promises, "If we confess our sins, he is faithful and just and will forgive us our sins and purify us from all unrighteousness"

(1 John 1:9). That means if we ask God to forgive us from past sins, he does. Period. "As far as the east is from the west, so far has he removed our transgressions from us" (Psalm 103:12). The Bible also promises, "There is now no condemnation for those who are in Christ Jesus," (Romans 8:1). God gives us grace that we don't deserve and can't earn. It is there for the asking.

If reading about the Shulammite's plea for her friends to wait is causing your heart to hurt because of the time (or times) you didn't wait, stop right now and ask God to forgive you of your past sexual encounters. And then believe that he has. You are a dearly loved child of God who has been forgiven for your sins, cleansed by Christ's blood, and made new by Christ's resurrection power. Don't let the Devil condemn you for what Jesus has already forgiven you for.

If you have asked for God's forgiveness and are still feeling condemned, know that condemnation is not coming from God. Our Enemy is called "the accuser of our brothers and sisters, who accuses [us] before our God day and night" (Revelation 12:10). "She did this and she did that," he hisses. And God replies, "Really? I don't remember."

> We cannot go back and make a new start, but we can start now and make a new ending.

However, if you're feeling convicted, that's another story. The Holy Spirit convicts us of sin in order to convince us to turn away from sin. That's what Jesus did with the woman caught in adultery in John 8. The religious leaders wanted to condemn her to death, but Jesus offered forgiveness to set her free. He didn't sugarcoat her sin; he acknowledged it, offered forgiveness for it, and told her to leave her life of sin—to stop having the affair. When you come to Christ, his righteousness becomes yours. Isn't that the most amazing news ever? He is able to make all things new, and that includes you and me.

God wants you to have the best marriage possible. He wants you to have the best sex imaginable. God doesn't want you to bring your past baggage into your present bedroom. Give it to him. Live fully and freely with your mister. The best is yet to be.

The Invitation to Lifelong Love

Romantic relationships tend to progress with predictable milestones. In chapter 2 Solomon was ready to take the next step and present the Shulammite to his family and friends. I can still remember the first time I met the Jaynes clan. It was a Thanksgiving at Steve's Aunt Julie's house. About fifty-five relatives filtered through the doors with vegetable casseroles, roasted turkeys, and enough pies and pastries to fill a bakery. It was a bit overwhelming. These were his people.

I faced questions from Steve's cousins, skeptical eyeballing from his mom, and wary glances from his siblings. Did I mention *skeptical*?

It sounds like the Shulammite's introduction to King Solomon's clan was a little bit more positive as he made what had once been a private relationship a public one. She certainly felt good about it. The Shulammite didn't have to worry that Solomon was ashamed of her humble beginnings or that he wanted to keep their relationship a secret. He made his intentions perfectly clear when he took her home to meet the family.

> Let him lead me to the banquet hall,
> and let his banner over me be love. (Song 2:4)

I love how another translation interprets her words: "It's obvious how much he loves me" (NLT). Yes, meeting the family takes any relationship to a deeper level, and these two were ready.

Shortly after that celebration, they separated for a time. Most likely he returned to the palace and she to her home in Shumen. But then the snow of winter (their time apart) melted, and the spring came again. Solomon was on the move.

> Listen! My beloved!
> Look! Here he comes,
> leaping across the mountains,
> bounding over the hills.
> My beloved is like a gazelle or a young stag
> Look! There he stands behind our wall,
> gazing through the windows,
> peering through the lattice. (vv. 8–9)

Solomon was leaping across the mountains and bounding over the hills like a giddy schoolboy. But he was no boy. He was a hunky man—as muscular and virile as a young stag, frisky and excited.

When Steve and I were dating, he had an old beige Volkswagen Beetle with no air conditioning, no seat belts, and no speedometer. Yes, it would be illegal today. One thing the old jalopy did have was a distinct sound to the engine—like a go-cart. Whenever I heard his Bug pull up to my apartment, my heart skipped a beat. That's what we see with the Shulammite as her man came back after a time apart. She saw him coming, and she couldn't wait!

At the same time, it seems the Shulammite was still struggling with her insecurities, so she was hiding. "Look! There he stands behind our wall, gazing through the windows, peering through the lattice," she said. There's something a little scary about love during the dating days, don't you think? *Is he serious? Will this grow into marriage? Am I hearing God correctly? What am I doing? What are his intentions? What if we do get married? Will it last?*

Solomon was calling her to come out from hiding so he could reassure her that he wasn't going anywhere. He was taking the initiative, not standing by idly, as Adam did in the garden of Eden when Eve conversed with the serpent. He was taking charge, something we women love in a man of strong character, and I imagine her heart was pounding in her chest.

> My beloved spoke and said to me,
> "Arise, my darling,
> my beautiful one, come with me.
> See! The winter is past;
> the rains are over and gone.
> Flowers appear on the earth;
> the season of singing has come,
> the cooing of doves
> is heard in our land.
> The fig tree forms its early fruit;
> the blossoming vines spread their fragrance.
> Arise, come, my darling;
> my beautiful one, come with me." (vv. 10–13)

Solomon's pursuit of the hiding Shulammite reminds me of my mom and the spring she experienced in the winter of her life. She and my father had a very rocky marriage from the start. They tied the knot when she was eighteen and he was nineteen, and the fighting started soon after. Dad had a drinking problem and what we'd call today "intermittent rage disorder." The years of alcohol-induced rage left Mom bitter, angry, and resentful. It seemed she simply survived life and never seemed to enjoy it. She was very attractive and had plenty of material possessions, but her heart was empty.

Both of my parents did become Christians later in life, but still, they never experienced much joy in their marriage. When my dad was fifty-six years old, he was diagnosed with Alzheimer's disease, and I watched a strong, vibrant man turn into a person who was unable to feed himself, bathe himself, or walk by himself. As my mother cared for him, what little light was in her eyes went almost completely dim. Ten years after the initial diagnosis, my father passed away.

Not too long after my dad died, my mother met a wonderful man, Pete Wright. Pete said he had never seen someone as pretty as my mom with so much sadness in her eyes. He decided he would make it his mission to change that. He pursued her, won her affection, and rekindled that light that had been snuffed out by pain. Pete was one of the sweetest, kindest, gentlest men I had ever known.

For the first time in my life, I saw my mother truly happy. She had met Mr. (W)right and transformed before my very eyes. It was springtime in the winter of her life. The sun shone brighter, her steps were lighter, and her eyes danced with excitement and joy. Suddenly I was a better daughter (even though I had not changed a bit), and her friends were kinder (even though they had not changed one iota). Life was just better all the way around. As Samuel Taylor Coleridge wrote, "What was the first effect of love, but to associate the feeling with every object in nature—the trees whisper, the roses exhale their perfumes, the nightingales sing, the very sky seems in unison with the feeling of love: it gives to every object in nature a power of the heart."[14]

For the first time in her life, my mom felt completely loved, cherished, and adored. Pete had wooed her with words, just as Solomon had wooed his Shulammite. When she and Pete were married, she wore a rhinestone tiara. How appropriate.

When I think about the Shulammite, and all of us in the early days of love, I think of the newness of spring. Solomon surely did. He beckoned his *rayati* to romp through the fields bursting with new life. The words captured the beauty of the season and the excitement of their love as the black and white of winter gave way to the radiant color of spring.

Many commentators think this could be when Solomon actually proposed to the Shulammite. He asked her to come away with him—twice. But even with all her longing and desire, she seemed to be a bit hesitant. He was everything she'd ever dreamed of, but when fantasy became a reality, she froze.

Here's what I love about Solomon: he didn't give up! He came bounding over the hills to see the Shulammite, and even when she suddenly became hesitant, he continued pursuing her.

> O my dove, in the clefts of the rock,
>   in the crannies of the cliff,
> let me see your face,
>   let me hear your voice,
> for your voice is sweet,
>   and your face is lovely. (v. 14 ESV)

Solomon didn't just want to talk to the Shulammite. He wanted to listen to her. Listening is a big part of any courtship and a building block for any marriage. That's how we learn about the other person. If we're the one doing all the talking, then we're not learning anything about the one we're talking to. When I met Steve I wanted to know everything about him. I wanted to know about his childhood, his hopes for the future, his fears, and his faith. I wanted to know little intricate details: his favorite foods, books, and movies. The feeling was mutual; Steve had identical questions for me. Solomon wanted to know about the Shulammite in the same way.

Later in this book we're going to look at the power of a couple's words. Tethered to the power of words spoken is the power of listening—really listening. A couple who has lasting intimacy is a couple who has learned to communicate beyond the surface of verbal exchange necessary for daily function. Great listeners don't simply listen with their ears; they listen with their entire beings.

We listen with our eyes as we make eye contact to show that we're paying attention. This lets our spouses know that they are more important than anything else at the moment. They have our full attention. If Steve starts to tell me something, and I don't stop what I'm doing but say, "Go on, I'm listening," he'll doubt that I really am. You can't listen well and multitask at the same time.

We listen with our facial expressions to let our spouses know we're engaged in a positive way—not judging or condemning. Our faces don't say, *Hurry up and finish this story so I can get back to what I was doing.* They don't say, *I'm not really interested in what happened between Bob and Brad at work.* The wise wife's facial expression says, *Tell me more. There's no one in the world I would rather listen to than you.*

We listen with our minds by asking good questions when our husbands are telling us about something that is on their hearts. Responses such as "I'm so sorry that happened," "How did that make you feel?" and "What happened next?" show that you're listening and inviting deeper conversation. Judging responses such as "You shouldn't have said that," "You shouldn't feel that way," or "I think you're wrong" will shut down the conversation and lock down his heart. That husband will wish he'd kept his mouth shut and be reluctant to voice his feelings in the future.

We listen with our hearts by listening beyond the words spoken, to the hurt behind them. Are your spouse's words being filtered through the sieve of a hurtful past? Are your husband's words tainted by past abuse or trauma? Rejection or abandonment? Sexual exploitation or shameful experimentation? Dig deeper to move beyond the words to discover the wounds. You might be God's instrument in his ultimate healing.

One husband told me this about his longing for his wife to listen to him: "One of our biggest struggles in our marriage has been communication. I tend to hold things in for two reasons. One, I don't want to bother her as she has enough on her plate. And two, when I do communicate, the response seems to be negative, or I get a lot of advice when all I want is a listening ear."

Another man shared the following: "One thing I wish my wife understood better about me is my desire to have her listen to me—really listen, not only with her ears, but with her mind. I want her to understand me when I talk and explain things to her. I want her to work with me, not against me—to be my partner, not my antagonist. I want her support and cooperation, not a challenge."

Above all, your husband needs to know that you are his safe place. He needs to have absolute confidence that no matter what he tells you, you will not repeat it to someone else, you will not judge him because of his feelings, and you will never think less of him for his story. Wrap his words in the tender blanket of your understanding and love. His ability to open up to you will be determined by your compassionate reaction and unconditional acceptance.

Yes, men and women are different, but when it comes to being listened to, we're from the same planet. Contemporary stereotypes would say that women are more interested in emotional intimacy than men, while men are more interested in physical intimacy than women. Isn't it interesting that so far we've seen the Shulammite be the one showing the most interest in the physical aspects of the relationship and Solomon being the one who wanted her to come out from behind the cleft and have a conversation?

His ability to open up to you will be determined by your compassionate reaction and unconditional acceptance.

You might feel that I've deviated from the theme of lifelong intimacy, but here's the deal: honest, open communication is the catalyst for a meaningful sexual relationship. When we share our hearts, we are more inclined to share our bodies. It is extremely difficult to be sexually intimate with a spouse who is emotionally frigid or verbally aloof.

When was the last time you sat down with your husband, asked him good questions, and really listened to his heart? I'm not talking about questions that can be answered with one-word answers such as yes or no, but heart-searching or soul-revealing questions. Many times men get nervous when you say you want to talk, because they fear you want to discuss some problem in the relationship or a flaw in his manhood. Make sure that when you do initiate conversation, you're not doing it just to fuss at him; come to him with a desire to learn what's on his heart. Then when he answers, listen with your whole being.

C. S. Lewis wrote, "Eros will have naked bodies; friendship naked personalities."[15] It is in the sharing and the listening that friendship is born. Getting to know each other doesn't stop after the dating phase is over. At the time of this writing, I've been married to Steve for thirty-eight years, and I haven't stopped learning new things about him, nor he about me. Why? Because we are still asking good questions and listening with our entire beings: our eyes, our facial expressions, our minds, and, most importantly, our hearts.

My Beloved Is Mine

Even though the Shulammite all of a sudden became a bit shy about her outward demonstration of affection, her inward desire was still just as strong as ever. Solomon's continual pursuit of her heart, even in her hesitancy, made her love him even more.

> My beloved is mine and I am his;
> he browses among the lilies.
> Until the day breaks
> and the shadows flee,
> turn, my beloved,
> and be like a gazelle
> or like a young stag
> on the rugged hills. (vv. 16–17)

Nine times Solomon refers to the Shulammite as "mine." He didn't mean it in a domineering way, as if he owned her, but in a loving way, because she had given herself to him. There is a sense of equality in the Shulammite's words, "My beloved is mine and I am his." They knew they belonged to each other and with each other.

Notice that she called him a shepherd that browses among the lilies. I love that she saw him not as a king to rule over her but as a shepherd to care for her, love her, and guide her tenderly. And those lilies? That's code for her body. We'll see that imagery come up time and time again.

All of this pondering stirred up sexual longings once again. The girl dreamed about a time when he would make love to her and they would revel in an entire night of passion. She pictured her future husband as a virile, strong stag friskily navigating the mountainous terrain of her body. I have a feeling she didn't let him know how she was feeling but kept it to herself. Let's see why. Page-turner!

Chapter 3

Little Foxes and Pesky Fears

If the Song of Solomon were a Broadway play, then it would need to stop right here for an intermission and a scenery change. In chapter 3 of the Song, everything was about to change. The everyday fields would give way to extravagant flamboyance. The Shulammite was getting dressed in her bridal gown, and Solomon was placing the finishing details on the processional. Let's give the stagehands a moment to set up for the Grand Celebration—the wedding. Meanwhile, we'll talk about foxes and fears.

In chapters 1 and 2 of the Song, we caught a snapshot of the initial attraction, growing love, and deepening desire in the courtship between Solomon and his Shulammite. The closer their relationship grew, the more difficult time apart became. The poetic symbolism we've read is sensual yet modest. Nothing about the words has been crude or crass. At the same time, there is no doubt that these two lovers couldn't wait for the moment when they could give themselves fully and freely to one another.

Even though the couple was lovestruck beyond reason, they were not blind to the potential problems that could sneak into any relationship.

Catch for us the foxes,
    the little foxes
that ruin the vineyards,
    our vineyards that are in bloom. (Song 2:15)

Theologians are not sure if these are the words of Solomon or the Shulammite. Either way, the words speak of watching out for, and capturing, anything that could sneak in and ruin the budding vineyard of their love.

The morning of our wedding, I had the same concern. As I looked in the mirror, an unwelcomed thought interrupted my daydreaming. *Steve is everything I ever dreamed of: handsome, smart, ambitious, strong, and godly. But doesn't every bride feel this happy and in love on her wedding day? What could possibly go wrong in other marriages that cause so many couples to call it quits? Are we that different from the thousands of couples who have walked the aisle before us?* I didn't call them foxes, but I prayed right then and there that God would show us anything or anyone that could sneak in our marriage and sully our love.

Finally, I put my musing aside and gathered with my bridesmaids, a handful of older women, and a few close family members. The bridesmaid brunch was a bouquet of toile tablecloths, yellow roses, and fine china intended to make us feel like princesses headed to the ball.

Speaking of a ball, what was my husband doing at the same time the women nibbled and giggled with thoughts of a day filled with fairy-tale romance? He and his groomsmen were playing a sweaty, aggressive, competitive game of basketball a few blocks away. Roy Thomas had a basketball goal nailed to an old splintery telephone pole at the end of his driveway. The guys laced up their sneakers and separated into teams of shirts and skins. For two hours they shot hoops, called fouls, and high-fived.

Later that night, I sat on the edge of the bed doing something I'd never thought I'd be doing on my honeymoon. I poked and prodded a needle in Steve's hand to remove a splinter that had lodged under his skin when he slam-dunked the basketball a few hours earlier.

Little splinters can be painful. They're certainly distracting. If they aren't removed quickly they can fester and cause infection. It's the same way with the "little foxes" that Solomon warned about in chapter 2.

Vineyards bloom in late spring, and the fruit isn't ready to be harvested until late summer. By then the grapes have been sweetened by the sun and plumped by the rain; they're mature and ready to be picked. Solomon's reference to the "vineyards that are in bloom" lets us know that their love was still in the courting stage. But, just as little foxes can sneak in and ruin a blooming relationship, they can also creep in and wreck a mature marriage.

Foxes are stealthy and devious little animals that steal eggs from chicken coops, vegetables from gardens, and, in this case, grapes from vines. They actually love the tender buds that form before the grapes emerge. Even though they are small and seemingly insignificant animals, left unrestrained and unfettered, they can ruin an entire crop.

In the same way, Solomon was on the lookout for anything that could sneak in and sabotage the blooming vineyard of their love. In most relationships it isn't the big problems that tear a couple apart but the daily deterioration from little annoyances that chip away at the firm foundation and ruin intimacy.

> Just as little foxes can sneak in and ruin a blooming relationship, they can also creep in and wreck a mature marriage.

So what are the little foxes that sneak into and attempt to destroy a relationship? Here are a few: disrespect, dishonesty, jealousy, complacency, irresponsibility, guilt, selfishness, mistrust, self-centeredness, bitterness, poor communication, anger, or irritating habits. Foxes could be too much time at the office, too little time alone as a couple, too many hours reclining with the remote, or too many nights cuddled up with a good book.

Those are the ones you would expect to undermine a relationship, but here are few others that might not seem as obvious: making motherhood a priority above the marriage, serving the church more than serving your mate, caring more about a spotless house or an weedless lawn than a happy spouse. The truth is, the list of little foxes is endless, and every couple will have their own version. A little fox is anything or anyone that could potentially sneak into your marriage to eat away at the fruit of lifelong love and intimacy.

One in particular that I've struggled with is similar to what the Shulammite struggled with. Remember, at the end of chapter 2 she was hiding in the cleft of a rock. When Steve and I were dating, I had a tendency to hide as well. Not literally, but emotionally. I was afraid of conflict—I had seen too much of it in my home. When Steve and I had a disagreement, I would frequently shut down. But he called to me as Solomon called to the Shulammite to come out of the cleft, to open up and talk about what was bothering me. Steve knew that my tendency to withdraw was a little fox that could cause big problems in the long run, so we had to deal with it early on.

Maybe you've noticed a little fox that keeps creeping into your relationship when you least expect it. The best thing we can do is to pick up on its scent before it sneaks through the front door. Sniff out the tendency to control, the proclivity toward jealousy, the propensity to pout, the bent to bully, the inclination to intimidate or manipulate.

You wouldn't expect a cute little fox darting about in a massive vineyard to cause much trouble. I'd be more prone to think, *Oh, he's just a cute little thing. So what if he eats a few grapes?* But with that attitude in marriage, the next thing you know a few grapes ends up being an entire vineyard, and you end up with not a grape of admiration, respect, or love on the vine. There's certainly not a lot of hugging and kissing going on in a vineyard that's been picked clean.

Solomon recognized the Shulammite's tendency to hide and its potential to cause trouble. But he didn't run away from it; he worked through it. Solomon continued pursuing her and let her know that he wasn't going anywhere.

Did you notice that Solomon said, "Catch *for us* the foxes" (v. 15)? Who was he talking to? "Catch for us" sounds as if he were asking someone else to catch the foxes. I think Solomon was whispering a prayer, asking God to help them both recognize and remove anything that could damage their relationship. He was petitioning God to protect and preserve their love, as we all should.

It can be easy to ignore the little foxes. But eventually they will nip at our happy heels. If they aren't dealt with, little foxes become big foxes with fangs of disappointment and claws of resentment. Yes, foxes come in all shapes and sizes, from dysfunction to dissatisfaction, selfishness to possessiveness, jealousy to flippancy. The key is to catch them while they're still little before they have time to tear the marriage apart.

Pre-wedding Jitters

As I mentioned earlier, many scholars think that Solomon proposed at the end of chapter 2. If that's the case, the Shulammite didn't give him an answer. We have no indication that she accepted either of his invitations to come away with him. Perhaps that's why chapter 3 begins with the Shulammite's disturbing dream about possibly losing her man.

> All night long on my bed
> I looked for the one my heart loves;
> I looked for him but did not find him.
> I will get up now and go about the city,
> through its streets and squares;

I will search for the one my heart loves.
So I looked for him but did not find him.
The watchmen found me
as they made their rounds in the city.
"Have you seen the one my heart loves?" (3:1–3)

Have you ever had one of those dreams that seemed to go on and on and on? Scientists say that dreams can last for a few seconds, or approximately twenty to thirty minutes.[1] I've dreamed entire mini-series. Sometimes I wake up during a disturbing dream, and when I fall back asleep, the story seems to pick back up where it left off. I think that's what we see happening to our friend. She had been dreaming "all night long on [her] bed."

In the dream she frantically searched for the one her heart loved. You can almost feel the panic as she ran down the streets. "Have you seen him? Have you seen him?" she asked everyone she encountered. She feared she'd lost him.

The night watchmen were like city guards who patrolled the streets and city walls. She asked them if they had seen the one her heart loved, which was the way she referred to him not once, not twice, but four times in the first four verses of this chapter. It literally means "the one my soul loves." She loved him with her mind, will, and emotions—her entire soul. The fact that she didn't actually say his name made it seem more dreamlike. In the dream sequence the watchmen didn't give an answer, and she kept searching.

It is common for a woman to feel a sense of panic at some point during the dating or engagement period. *Does he feel about me the same way I feel about him? Suppose I let him know how I feel about him and then he leaves me? Am I pretty enough? Am I what he's looking for? What will he think when he finds out about my past? What will he think when he meets my crazy family?*

Those fears don't stop when the couple gets married. We gals look in the mirror and wonder if we have what it takes for the long haul. We question how we measure up to the women at his workplace. We question whether we're sexy enough, exciting enough, or interesting enough to hold our husbands' interest. We wonder if we will become a statistic. *Will he still love me when my tummy pooches and my skin sags? What if he gets tired of me? Will I make him happy? Will he make me happy? Have I married the wrong person?*

If you've been married for more than a few days, then you have most likely figured out that the blessed union doesn't stay so blessed without a lot of work. And, I daresay, the most important "work" we can do as wives is on our knees. The psalmist wrote, "Unless the LORD builds the house, the builders labor in vain. Unless the LORD watches over the city, the guards stand watch in vain" (Psalm 127:1). Only God can truly protect your marriage and your man. And he invites you to participate in the unleashing of his power by praying for your husband and turning the key to the storehouse of heaven's door for blessings outpoured.

Every wife will eventually come to the realization that she does not have it in her power to make marriage work. It is only through the power of God working in both the husband and the wife to make the intertwined strand of three cords unbreakable. Through prayer, our fears will fade as God's power and provision permeate our relationship. No matter where your marriage is on a continuum of terrific to tolerable to terrible, prayer can make a bad marriage good and a good marriage great. Prayer is the conduit through which God's power is released and his will is brought to earth as it is in heaven. And God's will for your marriage is for it to thrive for a lifetime of emotional, spiritual, and physical intimacy.

Finally, the Shulammite finds her man:

> Scarcely had I passed them
> when I found the one my heart loves.

I held him and would not let him go
    till I had brought him to my mother's house,
    to the room of the one who conceived me. (Song 3:4)

I can envision the Shulammite's heart pounding as her bad dream came to an end and she embraced her man. He probably laughed at her unfounded fear and hugged her right back.

> Through prayer, our fears will fade as God's power and provision permeate our relationship.

The Shulammite dreamed of taking Solomon to her mother's house, and that part of the dream came true. It was Hebrew custom for a girl to live with her parents until she married, so this would have been her house as well. This shows that she was not dreaming of a premarital sexual encounter, but one that her family supported. Not until the wedding day would she leave the security of her mother's home to be with her husband. So even though she might have been hesitant when Solomon was calling her to come out from hiding in the cleft, she was now truly ready to become his bride.

All fear of the future was gone. Now she knew she didn't want to live without him one more day. As it's been said, "When choosing a marriage partner, it's sound advice to select not just someone you can live with but someone you cannot live without."[2] She had found her person, and she wasn't about to let him go.

Chapter 4

Saying "I Do" and Meaning "I Will"

The stagehands had now finished the scene change. The dusty fields, apple trees, and banqueting hall had been replaced with a custom-crafted carriage of gold and silver inlay, sixty armored swordsmen, and a host of adoring spectators. The curtain rose to the most magnificent wedding ceremony the world had ever seen. Solomon and his Shulammite were now poised and ready to become man and wife at last.

Think back to your wedding day. If you're like most folks, you have the day chronicled minute by minute with photographs, videos, Facebook, and Instagram. Weddings are the singular time in a couple's life when the people they love most are all gathered together at one time and place. Then there are the flowers, the dresses, the matching suits or tuxedoes, the music, the dancing, the food . . . what a day! A survey by the Knot showed that the average cost of a wedding in the United States in 2016 was $35,329.[1] I'm not going to comment on that, except that the words *house down payment* come to mind.

In chapter 3 of the Song of Solomon, the big day finally arrived. Solomon spared no expense to make this the most memorable day of his bride's life. As I mentioned, if the Song of Solomon were a Broadway play, this would be the second act right after the intermission when new props have been added to the scene. If it were a movie, the screen would turn from black to bursting with color!

Here they came!

> Who is this coming up from the wilderness
>   like a column of smoke,
> perfumed with myrrh and incense
>   made from all the spices of the merchant?
> Look! It is Solomon's carriage,
>   escorted by sixty warriors,
>   the noblest of Israel,
> all of them wearing the sword,
>   all experienced in battle,
> each with his sword at his side,
>   prepared for the terrors of the night.
> King Solomon made for himself the carriage;
>   he made it of wood from Lebanon.
> Its posts he made of silver,
>   its base of gold.
> Its seat was upholstered with purple,
>   its interior inlaid with love.
> Daughters of Jerusalem, come out,
>   and look, you daughters of Zion.
> Look on King Solomon wearing a crown,
>   the crown with which his mother crowned him
> on the day of his wedding,
>   the day his heart rejoiced. (Song 3:6–11)

The Song painted a beautiful picture of a fragrant smoke billowing, muscular soldiers marching, golden swords glistening, purple robes flowing, hand-cut jewels shimmering, and young women straining on tiptoes to catch a glimpse of the bride. Just a short time ago, the

Shulammite was a humble field hand working under the scornful eye of the scorching sun. She'd had no time to take care of her appearance or prepare for her future. And then Solomon had plucked her from the field and placed her in the palace. Don't you know her head was swimming? I often wonder about her mean old stepbrothers. There's no mention of them at the wedding, but I bet they were cowering in the crowd, hoping Solomon wouldn't string them up by their toenails.

For months Solomon had wooed the Shulammite with the easy tenderness of a shepherd rather than the egotistic toughness of a king. He hadn't coerced her with his power but pursued her with his love. And yet everything about the wedding procession reflected the power and strength of the man: cedars of Lebanon, purple royal fabric, gold and silver posts, and sword-bearing groomsmen.

When my nephew Jonathan got married, he had so many friends that it was difficult for him to choose who would be in the wedding party. He selected eight to be groomsmen, six to be ushers, and eight more to sit on the front row as "men of honor." But Solomon surpassed even Jonathan. He had sixty groomsmen in his processional. These guys weren't wearing boutonnieres and seating female attendees. They strapped on swords, ready to fight off anyone who dared interfere with the big day. It was common for bandits and thieves to hide out and attack a royal procession. Solomon made sure his bride was safe and secure. Don't you know she felt totally protected and cherished as sixty warriors flanked her carriage?

When it comes to sexual intimacy, a woman needs to know that she is safe. We'll get to that more in the next chapter, but here we see that even before the wedding night, Solomon showed his bride that he would do everything in his power to make sure she felt secure.

If there's one thing we know about Solomon, it's that he could be extravagant. He'd gone all out to make this a day his bride would never forget. If she hadn't known before, she would see now just how important she was to him. Talk about a wedding party!

Also, did you notice that Solomon *made* the wedding carriage? He left nothing to chance by removing his royal robe and tying on a carpenter's apron. Hammer. Saw. Nails. Splinters. Nicks. Sweat. I wonder if he even slipped and banged his fingers a time or two. The materials used to build the wedding carriage—the wood imported from Lebanon, the silver posts, the gold base—were very similar to the materials used to build Solomon's temple. Both were crafted to perfection. Both glorified God. But here's the line that grabs my heart: "Its seat was upholstered with purple, its interior inlaid with love" (v. 10). Inlaid with love! What a guy!

This was certainly a lavish wedding ceremony. Princess Di or Meghan, the Duchess of Sussex, would have approved. I don't know about your wedding, but mine was nothing like any of these three. Even so, it was very precious to me.

Why do we have such elaborate wedding ceremonies? Is it just because we want to play dress-up and have a big party? Not a chance. Or at least I hope not. Getting married is the most important decision a person can make, other than joining oneself to Christ. Weddings put on display the most significant union between a man and a woman God ever created, the beginning of a covenant relationship that is meant to last a lifetime. And they invite loved ones to join in the couple's happiness. That's certainly a lot to celebrate. As we read about Solomon and the Shulammite's big day, I encourage you to remember yours.

The God-Ordained Purpose of Leaving and Cleaving

Remember when you stood at the back of the church or venue waiting to walk down the aisle? The music started, the attendees stood, and the mothers cried. A new family unit was about to be brought into existence. It was a departure from the old life and an entrance into the new. Solomon and the Shulammite's wedding may have looked different from yours and mine, but some of the same elements were mingled in.

At first glance, the prose in Song 3:6 reads as if Solomon were approaching his bride, but in the original Hebrew, the pronoun *who* is singular and feminine, telling us that it was the bride who was traveling from her home to the king's city for the wedding.[2] Twice Solomon said to the Shulammite, "Come with me" (2:10, 13), and now she was doing just that. She was leaving her people and being joined to her husband.

Did you notice also how, later in the passage, King Solomon was wearing a crown his mother had made (3:11)? It was customary in those days for a mother to make her son a crown for his wedding day. This was the crown that Solomon would have worn not as king of Israel but as king of his home.

Sometimes it's hard for a mama to take second place in her son's life when he gets married. In making Solomon a crown, his mother showed him that she heartily approved of his choice and would support them in every way. Solomon's mom was the woman who instructed her son with the words of Proverbs 31:10–31. Her actions seemed to say that he had found such a woman.

For centuries, crowning was a part of wedding ceremonies. "The bride was crowned with her veil, usually held in place by a heavily embroidered wedding cap or a crown of flowers. The wedding cap was perceived to be provided for her by her father—in essence, the father was crowning his daughter for marriage. The groom was crowned with a simple band of gold or with a garland of flowers, usually by his mother."[3] Today the tradition continues with the father walking his daughter down the aisle and giving his little girl to the groom while the mother of the groom watches with a tissue in hand.

In the garden of Eden, after fashioning Eve, God presented her to

Adam. Then he said, "Therefore shall a man leave his father and his mother, and shall cleave unto his wife: and they shall be one flesh" (Genesis 2:24 KJV). The ESV translates the word *cleave* as "hold fast" to his wife. The NIV says "is united" to his wife.

Cleave is a word we don't use much today. The Hebrew word is *dabaq* and means "to cling, stay close, cleave, stick with, follow closely, join to."[4] Like gluing two pieces of paper together, the couple is glued in such a way that if anyone were to try and pull them apart, pieces of one would cling to the other.

There cannot be a true bonding of souls if one or both of the partners in the marriage does not leave the family of origin. Leaving doesn't mean not having anything to do with the extended family, but it does mean that the most important family unit, the one that takes priority above all other earthly relationships, is between the new husband and wife. Just as a newborn baby cannot exist outside the womb until the cord is cut, a new couple cannot thrive outside the family of origin until the tether that has held them to their mother and father is severed.

Many marriages struggle because of the refusal to leave their parents and cleave to their spouses. When a man defers to his mother rather than his wife, it creates a wedge between him and his wife that God never intended. Likewise, when a wife confides in her mother rather than her husband, she is placing her mother in a position solely reserved for her husband. These are little foxes that can ruin the vineyard.

Two main trouble areas for couples who struggle with leaving and cleaving are dependency on parents for emotional and material support and allegiance to their parents over their spouses. Couples must not be afraid to establish healthy boundaries to keep their new family units a priority over their parents and siblings.

My husband has a twin brother, Dan. When the twins got married, Steve's parents struggled with letting go. They lived four hours away and often announced that they were coming for a visit without being invited. To make matters worse, there was no departing date mentioned. In their minds there was an open-door policy. They had the idea of *mi casa es su casa*, and *su casa es mi casa*. It wasn't that Steve and I weren't on the same page when it came to putting our relationship first; it was just that we didn't know how to handle his parents who refused to let go of their boys and allow them to form their own families.

Finally Dan and Steve set up a time to meet with their parents. With lists in hand they set out clear boundaries with the reasons why. It was excruciatingly painful for all four of them. Tearful parents. Guilt-ridden young men. "You don't love us anymore," their parents cried. Of course, that was not the case at all. The guys loved their parents very much. However, they knew that for their own marriages to survive and thrive someone had to cut the cord. Since their parents wouldn't do it, they were going to have to do it for them. If healthy limits had not been established, if leaving and cleaving had not taken place, the twins' marriages would have continued to suffer. Their parents had to come to grips with the fact that when it came to their married boys, *tu casa es tu casa*. Once the initial tension subsided, they adjusted to the new expectations. Years later they were thankful that both Steve and Dan had strong marriages that would last a lifetime. Every parent's dream.

Leaving can be painful for some couples. But I tell you this, there will be no cleaving if there is no leaving.

If you're holding this book as a mother-in-law, I encourage you to do everything you can to make it easy for your son or daughter to leave and cleave to his or her spouse. Help your adult child live guilt-free for creating family traditions that might not include you. Encourage your adult child to lean on his or her spouse for advice and support rather

There will be no cleaving if there is no leaving.

than on you. Give them gifts that foster a deeper connectedness, such as money for weekends away by themselves, date-night certificates, or babysitting for times alone. Never make your married child feel conscience-stricken for choosing his or her spouse over you. Better yet, never make your married child feel as if he or she *has* to choose at all.

Making a Covenant Versus Signing a Contract

Solomon and the Shulammite (and their parents) seemed to grasp the concept of leaving and cleaving very well. They also didn't have trouble remembering that beyond the fancy clothes and fairy-tale decor, there was something very important going on in their wedding ceremony—something holy.

A wedding is an earthly ceremony of a spiritual covenant between a man and a woman before God. Our culture has made a wedding into one big party, more of an event than an everlasting covenant. And while it is a time for celebration, if we miss the spiritual significance, then we've missed the true meaning. If we miss the true meaning, then we forfeit the underlying foundation for lifelong intimacy.

Solomon and the Shulammite understood the meaning of marriage. They didn't miss it at all. Let's go back to their wedding procession.

There came the bride, with a pillar of smoke leading the way. That pillar of smoke or incense would have undoubtedly reminded the Hebrew attendees of the God who led the children of Israel through the wilderness with a pillar of cloud by day and a pillar of fire by night (Exodus 13:18–22). They would have remembered how God brought them out of Egyptian slavery and into the promised land. While there might have been an extensive guest list for the wedding celebration, God's presence was leading the way. He was the One who had brought them together and would keep them together.

But just like the promised land for the Israelites, the promised land of marriage is not without its struggles. If we keep coming to God as a couple, however, he will help us through every one of them. A study that analyzed divorce rates among Christians found that 60 percent of those who never attended church had been divorced or were separated compared with only 38 percent of those who attended church weekly.[5] Another study showed that couples who pray together every day divorce at a rate of one out of ten thousand.[6] So having God at the center of any marriage helps hold it together for the long haul. Inviting God's presence into the wedding celebration is a great place to begin. Solomon's preparation of the wedding ceremony confirmed that he considered marriage a sacred moment with God leading the way.

Some refer to the wedding ceremony as the "sacrament of marriage." The word *sacrament* literally means "sacred moment." It is the sacred moment when three strands—husband, wife, and God—are intertwined into one cord. Author Mike Mason summarized it well: "Marriage is the closest bond that is possible between two human beings. That, at least, was the original idea behind it. . . . Socially, legally, physically, emotionally, every which way, there is just no other means of getting closer to another human being, and never has been, than in marriage."[7]

Every aspect of the two persons' lives merge into a single unit. They give up much of their independence and give to each other selflessly. That certainly doesn't sit well in our me-centered society. Most are more comfortable with the idea of "meet me halfway." The problem is, who gets to decide where the halfway mark is? The biblical idea of marriage is one where both partners give all they have to meet the needs of the other—100 percent.

I was speaking with a young woman who was living with her boyfriend, and I asked her why they hadn't gotten married.

"I don't need a piece of paper or a legal document to love someone," she replied.

Nope, you sure don't. But that's not what marriage is. It's not just the feeling of loving someone. It is a covenantal commitment *to* love someone. Living together without being married offers an easy way out of the relationship if it hits a rough spot, or if one of the parties decides he or she doesn't love the other after all. It says, "I love you, but not enough to close off all other options and commit for a lifetime. And it if doesn't work out, we can walk away. Let's just give it a try and see how it goes."

You might say, "Well, getting married doesn't ensure one of the parties won't leave either." And you're right. The way you view marriage, covenant or contract, will either strengthen or weaken your likelihood to beat the odds.

As Matt Chandler put it, "At a fundamental level, a contract is an agreement between two parties arranging an exchange of goods or services. One party agrees to provide something for the other in exchange for something else. For most of our contracts, that something else is money."[8] We sign contracts all the time: credit cards, cell phones, cable television, bank loans, employment. They all have stipulations; mainly, as long as you do your part, you will receive your benefit. Can you imagine actually saying that out loud to your spouse? "As long as you meet my needs, I'll meet yours, and we'll stay married."

Contracts are broken all the time. "According to the contract, if one party fails to live up to its end of the arrangement, the contract is broken and the arrangement is altered."[9] Sounds like modern-day marriage in a nutshell.

But marriage was never intended to be a contract between two people in which goods or services are exchanged for payment. It is not a business deal. It is a holy covenant, or a sacred bond, between a man and a woman instituted by and publicly entered into before God. A wedding is a sacred moment when a man and a woman vow to leave mother and father and cleave to one another until death. The ceremony is an outward and visible symbol of an inward and spiritual commitment. It's not the ceremony itself or the piece of paper making it legal that's going to make a marriage last.

I married Steve because I loved him. Now I love him because I married him. Regardless of how well he holds up his end of the deal, I'm in it until one of us meets Jesus face-to-face. And isn't that what God does with you and me? He loves us regardless of how well we hold up our end of the deal. This is a hard lesson. I don't mean to make it sound easy. But that's really the point; we shouldn't expect it to be easy. We've committed to love another person in every condition of life.

In sickness and in health
For richer and for poorer
When grumpy and gracious
When attentive or aloof
When passionate and put-out
When sloppy or spic and span

Nope, you won't hear that in the wedding vows. That would be too raw and honest for the festivities. But that's the truth of the matter. Covenantal language says, "We're in this together till death do us part, no matter what."

The idea of "covenant" was serious business in the Bible. The Hebrew word is *beriyth* or *berith* and means "a treaty, compact, or agreement between two parties." The actual Hebrew word doesn't mean "to make a covenant" but "to cut a covenant." In Genesis 15 God made a covenant with Abraham. He instructed Abraham to slaughter a heifer, a goat, and a ram. Then he laid out the slain animals with one half of the bodies on one side of a path and one half on the other. This created a bloody path between them. Then Abraham fell into a trance while God walked between the sacrifices in the form of a firepot and flaming torch, much like the flame that preceded Solomon's wedding party. The idea was that the person making the covenant—in this case, God—was pledging to fulfill his covenant promises. When a person made the walk, he was saying that if he failed to keep the covenant, his life would become like the slain animals. When God walked the path of blood, he made a covenant promise to Abraham to establish the Jewish nation and bless the earth through them, which he later did through Jesus Christ.

A path of blood sounds very gory to our twenty-first century senses. We don't have to kill our dinner before we prepare it anymore. But, even though people back in Abraham's day were more accustomed to blood, walking this path did show the seriousness of the covenant. As strange as it may seem, I think of the Old Testament covenant every time I see a bride and groom walk down the aisle of a wedding ceremony with well-wishers on each side. It's serious business.

Wedding vows are not a declaration of present love but a mutually binding promise of future love, regardless of changing circumstances or fluctuating feelings. It is more than a lifelong commitment to another person. It is a lifelong commitment to God regarding another person. At least that's the way God intended for it to be.

Romantic love, whether one realizes it not, always points back to God—the Creator of love itself. It's like the rays of the sun that shine upon your face—rays that cause you to look toward the Source, God himself. As C. S. Lewis noted, romantic love and sex are like "the scent of a flower we have not found, the echo of a tune we have not heard, news from a country we have never yet visited."[10] But if we could follow the echo to its origin, we would find it emanating from the Father.

This is what the happy couple in Song of Songs 3 knew. This is what they celebrated. And once the festivities were about to come to a close, they were ready to sing the most sensual verse they'd ever sung. And it'd be just as sacred as the one before it.

Chapter 5

Unlocking the Secret Garden

Solomon and the Shulammite had finally said their vows to God, made promises to each other, and enjoyed the celebration with family and friends. Then the moment they'd been waiting for had arrived. With festive chatter in the background, Solomon took his bride by the hand, led her into the wedding chamber, and guided her to the marriage bed covered with embroidered silk and tasseled pillows. Of course, we don't know what the room actually looked like, but considering he left nothing to chance for the wedding preparations, I suspect he left nothing to chance in the honeymoon suite either.

Can't you picture it? Lanterns casting a golden glow as shadows dance on the walls. Welcoming pillows waiting by the fireside. A decanter of wine sitting by a bowl of pomegranates, figs, and dates. A lovestruck couple. A hungry-for-love husband. A tentatively anxious bride.

Steve and I were poor college students when we said our "I dos." We actually had a yard sale to scrounge up enough money for a honeymoon. After the wedding we drove off in a borrowed car and headed to the North Carolina coast. We were both aware of the gravity of what we had just done by becoming husband and wife, but on the drive to our honeymoon, it was the gravity of what we were about to do that was foremost in our minds.

During the five-hour drive I started getting nervous. Steve just had a silly grin on his face and a heavy foot on the gas pedal. Anxious thoughts bounced around in my head like ping-pong balls in a spinning bingo cage.

I've wanted to make love with this man for months. I've had a hard time keeping my hands off him. I've been kissing him like a crazy woman. I couldn't wait until the honeymoon—I've thought about it all the time. And now I'm nervous? I'm scared? What's wrong with me?

Steve just kept driving and grinning. I didn't even want to know what conversation was going on in his head.

When the time came I slipped on my lacy gown and eased into the candlelit room to my waiting husband. A shyness crept over me that I wasn't expecting. I'll never forget how Steve held me in his arms and sang to me—an old song titled "I'm Gonna Do Beautiful Things for You" written by Toni Wine and Barry Mason about how a husband was going to give his new wife a beautiful life.[1] He's still been giving me a beautiful life ever since.

I don't know if Solomon actually sang to the Shulammite on their first night together as husband and wife, but I am certain his words made her heart sing.

If the Song of Songs hasn't made you blush yet, now might just be the time it does. For centuries young Jewish boys were not even permitted to read the Song of Solomon until the age of twelve. Some sources say they had to be thirty or married. Even today, in Orthodox homes, it can't be read until one has gone through bar or bat mitzvah.

We're about to find out why.

In chapter 4 we finally get to the honeymoon and the halfway mark of this love poem. Sandwiched between chapters 3 and 4, the couple is finally wed. We aren't privy to the actual wedding vows but instead skip right from the procession to the wedding night—the night the courtship would end and the marriage would begin.

Traditionally, while the couple would be in their honeymoon suite, the wedding celebration would still be going on nearby. The groom's best friend would be standing outside the bedroom door. Once the marriage was consummated, the groom would knock on the door to let everyone know the good news.

I'm so glad that's not a tradition in our culture. It almost makes me a little queasy thinking about it. On our honeymoon night Steve and I stopped by a fast-food restaurant before heading to the condominium. While there, I ran into someone from high school.

"What are you doing here?" he asked.

"I just got married today," I replied. "We're on the way to our honeymoon."

Then I turned twelve shades of red. I knew he knew what we would be doing in the next few hours. I was mortified. I can't imagine someone standing outside the bedroom door.

In some cases back in Solomon's day, after the consummation the bride and groom would rejoin their friends for the celebration that often lasted seven days. I like our idea of going *away* for a seven-day honeymoon much better.

Touching Her with Words

I wonder if the Shulammite was nervous like I was. I wonder if this young girl was somewhat overwhelmed by the enormity of what had just taken place. I wonder if visions of the cloud of incense, sixty swordsmen, and the gilded carriage still swirled in her mind. I wonder if she was just a little scared about what was about to take place next. I suspect she was.

By the way Solomon slowly and tenderly assured her with his words, I think he understood her timidity. Dreaming about physical intimacy is one thing. Actually engaging in it for the first time is another. Solomon took his time to make his bride feel totally loved, cherished, and safe. In chapters 1 and 2 of the Song, the bride admitted her insecurities (1:5–6; 2:1), and on their wedding night the groom blew them all away with poetic praises of her beauty. He began and ended this segment in Song 4 with these compliments.

First in verse 1:

> How beautiful you are, my darling!
> Oh, how beautiful!

And then in verse 7:

> You are altogether beautiful, my darling;
> there is no flaw in you.

Within these two bookends of admiration, Solomon described seven of his bride's beautiful features with a verbal bouquet. Seven was the Hebrew number of perfection, and he was assuring her that she was perfection to him. Some of the language may seem strange to us, but in their culture, it would have made perfect sense. Each of his descriptions had hidden meaning, a secret code that she would have clearly understood. When we understand not simply what the comparisons mean but what they would have meant to her, we'll realize how Solomon's choice of words was magical. The important thing for us to grab on to is that Solomon tenderly touched the Shulammite's heart with his words before he touched her body with his hands.

Solomon started at the top of her head and worked his way down.

> Your eyes behind your veil are doves.
> Your hair is like a flock of goats
> descending from the hills of Gilead. (4:1)

Solomon compared his Shulammite's eyes to a dove's, just as he did in chapter 2. The couple was about to engage in the most intimate act created by God, and it began with looking into each other's eyes.

Then he reached up and began to undress her by removing her wedding cap that held the veil in place. As he did, her long sweeping hair fell around her shoulders. Most Jewish women had dark, curly hair. He compared her tresses to the black-haired goats descending Mount Gilead. Again, not a compliment that would make you and me swoon, but it melted the Shulammite's heart. Solomon painted a picture of the goats' flowing hair as they ran down the mountain, a cascading waterfall shimmering in the sun and billowing in the breeze. In ancient Hebrew traditions a woman only let her hair down for her husband. Can't you picture Solomon loosening her hair, admiring the curls falling around her bare shoulders, then nuzzling his face in their softness?

> Solomon tenderly touched the Shulammite's heart with his words before he touched her body with his hands.

The Shulammite responded to her husband with a smile. How do we know? Solomon next comments on her beautiful teeth.

> Your teeth are like a flock of sheep just shorn,
> coming up from the washing.
> Each has its twin;
> not one of them is alone. (v. 2)

Her teeth were clean, literally "coming up from the washing." If you separate the teeth in the middle, right under the nose, each tooth has one just like it on the other side. The right and left sides of her teeth were mirror images, and she wasn't missing any. We might chuckle at this praise, but remember, back in their day, there were no six-month checkups at the dentist's office. No whitening strips for a dazzling smile. To have all of her teeth, and have them white, was a real treat! Even today, nothing is more alluring than a sparkling smile.

The picture of "coming up from the washing" would have brought a picture to mind for Solomon and his bride that was more than simply "clean." She would have understood the underlying emotions surrounding a sheep shearing. It "was a festive occasion; neighbors gathered from miles around for the celebration. The newly shorn sheep scurrying out of the water was a happy sight, bringing smiles to the adults and laughter from the children. Shulamith's bright, playful smile is like this—a picture of joy that makes Solomon smile like he's at a festival and laugh with the delight of a child."[2]

These are some of those code words that may seem odd to us but made perfect sense to the bride. Next Solomon moved to her lips. I think he was getting pretty excited at this point.

> Your lips are like a scarlet ribbon;
>   your mouth is lovely.
> Your temples behind your veil
>   are like the halves of a pomegranate. (v. 3)

Solomon loved her lips and her mouth. He loved kissing her and couldn't wait to kiss her some more. I think he gently placed his lips on hers at this point, or at least traced their outline with his fingertip. *Lips* and *mouth* are two different words in Hebrew. When Solomon and the Shulammite spoke of the mouth, as they did several times throughout the Song, they were referring to what lies beyond the lips. This was not a peck on the lips, but sensual, deep, tongue-engaged, open-mouth kissing.

Then he compared her temples to halves of pomegranates. The word translated "temples" includes the cheeks. Her cheeks were blushingly red, perhaps with excitement mingled with modesty. The red seed-filled pomegranates were considered an aphrodisiac for arousing sexual desire and a symbol of fertility. He could have chosen any red fruit to compare her cheeks to, but he purposely chose one with a hidden meaning that she would have understood.

Then he moved to her neck.

> Your neck is like the tower of David,
> built with courses of stone;
> on it hang a thousand shields,
> all of them shields of warriors. (v. 4)

A long, stately neck was a mark of beauty in the ancient world. It appears she wore beautiful necklaces around that graceful neck on her wedding day—necklaces that reminded Solomon of warriors' shields. Warriors hung their shields on the tower of David during times of peace. It could be that she wore traditional Egyptian necklaces that were layered and reached all the way down to her shoulders.[3]

On that day the bride's neck was tall and unashamed. Her inner strength mirrored her husband's. She was his equal. The bride was not embarrassed by her husband's words but drank them in as wine before a fine meal.

I love what pastor Tommy Nelson had to say about the bride's necklace:

> The "tower of David" was a military structure, and the mighty men in David's army hung their shields on its exterior during peace times. It was a dramatic expression to all the people in the land that David was prepared for war but was presently at peace. Women's necklaces at that time were often made of coins or hammered flat pieces of metal, row upon row like a multiple strand of pearls. The woman's necklace might very well have looked like David's

> tower, and she might very well have been like all that the tower symbolized—ready to spring into action to defend what she knew to be hers, and equally ready to be at complete peace with the man she loved.[4]

That is the beauty of sexual intimacy blessed by the Creator and untainted by shame. She was at complete peace with the man she loved. Solomon then moved to her breasts.

> Your breasts are like two fawns,
> like twin fawns of a gazelle
> that browse among the lilies. (v. 5)

Okay, ladies, this is not referring to the Old and New Testaments, as some scholars of yesteryear have conjectured. Solomon was slowly moving from his bride's eyes to her mouth to her neck to her breasts. He loved her breasts and was excited to get to see them finally! Notice how gentle he was with her—how tender, how slow. What a beautiful picture God gives us of a man taking his time with a virgin on her honeymoon.

Most likely Solomon's mention of a fawn or graceful deer was referring to the softness of her breasts—as soft as a young fawn's fur. He longed to hold and caress them. Like a gentle shepherd, he didn't run up and grab the fawns. He was careful not to frighten them away but moved slowly and methodically. His likening of her breasts to a fawn or a young gazelle also alluded to their youthful appearance. Notice he was browsing—taking his time. Think of when you browse in a bookstore or an art gallery. You're not in a hurry; you're just taking your time looking first at one item, then another. Solomon was browsing the beautiful bounty of his wife's body and taking his time doing it.

Let's go back to the garden of Eden for a moment. Can you picture

Adam waking up and seeing Eve for the first time? Finally, there was someone like him . . . but different. The curves. The flowing hair. The eyes. He was breathless. Mike Mason wrote, "The whole thing begins with a wondrous *looking*, a helpless staring, an irresistible compulsion simply to behold."[5] I don't think Adam calmly said, "This is nice. Thanks a lot, God." I think he shouted, "Oh, man! You've got to be kidding! This is mine?"

Mason wrote the following about looking at his wife's naked body in his book, *The Mystery of Marriage*:

> I still haven't gotten used to seeing my own wife naked. It's almost as if her body is shining with a bright light, too bright to look at for very long. I cannot take my eyes off her—and yet I must. To gaze too long or too curiously is, even with her, a breach of propriety, almost a crime. It is not like watching a flower or creeping up to spy on an animal in the wild. No, my wife's body is brighter and more fascinating than a flower, shier than any animal, and more breathtaking than a thousand sunsets. To me her body is the most awesome thing in creation. Trying to look at her, just trying to take in her wild, glorious beauty, so free and primal, so utterly unchanged since the beginning of time, I catch a small glimpse of what it means that men and women have been made in the image of God. If even the image is this dazzling, what must the Original be like?[6]

That's how Solomon must have felt as he slid the bridal robe off his wife's shoulders. It was an echo of Adam's experience in the garden. Wondrously looking. Helplessly staring. Irresistible compulsion simply to behold. She was more than just a beautiful woman; she was a woman like no other he had ever seen. His words were a prelude to sexual intimacy, not just because they aroused passion, but also because they framed his passion in loving respect for her being. Once he reached her breasts, he had to stop and take a break. He could go no farther.

I asked my husband, "What's so intriguing to men about a woman's breasts? They're just two mounds of flesh on her chest."

"They're a lot more than that!" he replied.

I still don't understand what's so seductive about a woman's breasts to her husband, but I do know why. God made him that way. Pastor J. D. Greear said in a sermon series on the Song of Songs, "A guy catches a little cleavage, and his whole thought pattern for the day is totally changed. There's no way you [women] understand what goes through our minds, because if you did, you'd never stop slapping us."[7] God made us different. That's why we are called "the opposite sex." This is just one of the many ways.

Enjoying His Wife's Glorious Terrain

Solomon took a deep breath when he stopped to enjoy his wife's breasts. He was overcome with sensual longing, and his passion took over. Next, he told her what he was planning on doing for the rest of the night.

> Until the day breaks
>   and the shadows flee,
> I will go to the mountain of myrrh
>   and to the hill of incense. (v. 6)

"Until the day breaks and the shadows flee . . ." Solomon was planning on enjoying his bride. All. Night. Long. I don't know if Solomon had the stamina, but he sure had the desire. Notice, these are the exact words the Shulammite said in 2:17 when she was daydreaming about making love with her man. Now her dream was coming true.

Notice Solomon mentioned "the mountain of myrrh" and "the hill of incense." Where have we heard about this mountain of myrrh before? Back in Song of Songs 1:13. The Shulammite said, "My beloved is to me a sachet of myrrh resting between my breasts." Way back when being with Solomon sexually was but a dream, she fantasized about him resting between her breasts. Now, on their wedding night, it was actually happening. Solomon would climb those fragrant hills and enjoy every moment of it.

Finally, Solomon took in his wife's naked body and came to this conclusion: "You are altogether beautiful, my darling; there is no flaw in you" (4:7). The Hebrew word *mum* is translated "flaw, defect, spot, or blemish." I love how the NLT translates verse 7: "You are altogether beautiful, my darling, beautiful in every way." Solomon wanted his wife to know he found her to be beautiful not only on the outside but also on the inside. Those are words every woman wants to hear.

When my friends Bill and Pam Farrel were on their honeymoon, Pam looked in the mirror and began criticizing her body, commenting on each area and pointing out her shortcomings. Bill was actually sitting on the bed and admiring his new wife when she started verbally bashing her body. As she commented on areas that she thought needed improving, Bill began to panic and grow a little bit angry. Pam was putting down his wife! She was undermining his choice in whom he married!

God, will you help me out? he prayed. *I'm about to get pretty angry with the woman I love the most. Is there something I can do to help?* As he closed out the prayer, a thought crossed his mind that he knew was better than anything he would have come up with on his own. *Hey, Bill, you could do a better job than that mirror is doing right now!*

Bill stood up, wrapped his arms around Pam, and told her to look straight into his eyes. She turned, and he very seriously and lovingly said, "I will be your mirror. My eyes will reflect your beauty. You are beautiful, Pamela. You are perfect, and if you ever doubt it, come and stand before me. The mirror of my eyes will tell you the true story.

You are perfect for me. And if I have to throw away every mirror in the house to get you to believe me, I will. From now on, let me be your mirror." Pam smiled at the man she loved.[8]

Isn't this what we all want to hear? From the time a little girl stretches on her tiptoes to get a peek in the mirror, she desires to be beautiful—perhaps like her mommy. I believe the dream to be beautiful is not just cultural but at the very core of womanhood.

Solomon, in all his wisdom, let the Shulammite know that regardless of how she saw herself, he thought she was the most beautiful woman he'd ever seen. And that made her love him even more. As he undressed his bride, he unveiled her beauty. She saw herself through the mirror of his eyes once again. I wonder if that was when she truly started to believe him.

Inviting His Bride on a Marvelous Journey

Solomon took a break from describing his bride's beauty and invited her on a wonderful journey. He knew what was about to happen to his body at the culmination of this experience, and he wanted her to experience it too.

> Come with me from Lebanon, my bride;
> come with me from Lebanon.
> Depart from the peak of Amana,
> from the peak of Senir and Hermon,
> from the dens of lions,
> from the mountains of leopards. (4:8 ESV)

In verse 8 Solomon called his Shulammite his "bride" for the first time. Within five verses he used the word five times (vv. 8–12). No doubt Solomon was excited to be able to call her that at last! Notice he called her to come with him. The question is, come where? He wasn't talking about going on a trip from Lebanon to his hometown. It was another destination he had in mind. Solomon was not selfishly thinking of his own sexual gratification and satisfaction; he wanted his wife to enjoy the same release as well. He was about to take a trip to the pinnacle of sexual ecstasy, and he wanted her to come along with him.

It is a myth that orgasm should come naturally for a woman. On the other hand, it is not the husband's sole responsibility. Reaching a climax takes some effort on the wife's part as well. Very few women get a view from the top of the mountain without taking the effort to make the climb. Soaking in a bubble bath. Wearing pretty lingerie. Setting the mood of the bedroom. These are just a few ways to engage your most important sex organ—your mind—before you slip beneath the sheets.

What we think about sex will determine whether we enjoy it or endure it. That's why this book is so important to me. I want you to see that physical intimacy is a God-given gift, and each time you enjoy making love to your husband, God cheers.

Tommy Nelson wrote, "A woman . . . gets ready for sexual intimacy through what she thinks and feels, and to a great extent, she thinks and feels the way a man leads her to think and feel. Nothing calms a woman's fears and excites her passions as much as having a man tell her how wonderful she is."[9]

But suppose you don't have a husband who is as good with words as Solomon. When it comes to the bedroom, most men aren't. That's when we need to take time to prepare our minds. Some women do that by marking times for intimacy on their calendars and doing a little planning ahead. It is a myth that the best lovemaking is spontaneous. Many who are waiting for the spontaneous magic moment end up just simply waiting. When you take the time to plan ahead, and let your husband know that you're looking forward to your time together, he thinks he's the luckiest guy on earth! Not only does your husband want to be wanted, he wants you to enjoy sex as well.

Did you know that your husband longs to see you sexually fulfilled? His heart races when he sees you respond to his advances. It's really not all about him. It's about you too. He wants to know that he is the one who can take you to the moon and back with the crescendo or climax he created. After a wife has experienced earth-shaking ecstasy, her husband thinks to himself, *I did that to her, thank you very much!* As Dr. Kevin Leman, the author of *Sheet Music*, wrote, "There isn't a husband on this planet who doesn't want to know he can make his woman go crazy in bed."[10] Leman also stated, "Even more than your husband wants to have sex with you for his own sexual relief, the truth is, he wants to please you even more than he wants to be pleasured. It might seem like it's all about him, but what he really wants, emotionally, is to see how much you enjoy the pleasure he can give you. If he fails to do that, for any reason, he'll end up feeling inadequate, lonely, and unloved. Most of us men want to be our wives' heroes."[11]

Solomon wanted to be his wife's hero. He invited her to take the climb, and he was more than happy to help her get there.

Surrendering the Key to Her Private Garden

Solomon had to catch his breath after enjoying his wife's breasts, but he wasn't quite finished praising his bride and caressing her with his words.

> You have captivated my heart, my sister, my bride;
> you have captivated my heart with one glance of your eyes,
> with one jewel of your necklace.

How beautiful is your love, my sister, my bride!
How much better is your love than wine,
and the fragrance of your oils than any spice!
Your lips drip nectar, my bride;
honey and milk are under your tongue;
the fragrance of your garments is like the fragrance of Lebanon. (vv. 9–11 ESV)

Solomon moves from looking to tasting, to smelling, to touching, reminding us that sex involves all the senses because God made us that way. If you remember, in chapter 1, the Shulammite compared her beloved's kisses to wine and his fragrance to perfume poured out. Now Solomon was doing the same.

It might seem rather odd for Solomon to call his wife his sister, but in Near East poetry, *sister* was a term of endearment for one's wife. The inference was that the new wife was now related to her husband as closely as a blood relative.

Just as the pillar of smoke in the wedding processional reminded the wedding party of God's presence leading the children of Israel out of Egypt, Solomon now compared his wife's kisses to the choicest fruit of the promised land. She was God's promised land to him, flowing with milk and honey. That promised land had been like a locked-up garden, but she was about to hand over the key.

You are a garden locked up, my sister, my bride;
you are a spring enclosed, a sealed fountain.
Your plants are an orchard of pomegranates
with choice fruits,
with henna and nard,
nard and saffron,
calamus and cinnamon,
with every kind of incense tree,

with myrrh and aloes
and all the finest spices.
You are a garden fountain,
a well of flowing water
streaming down from Lebanon. (vv. 12–15)

Gardens were a beautiful metaphor in Hebrew poetry. Israel is an arid land. Before modern irrigation, gardens only grew around a water source. They were places of rest and refreshment in a hot, dusty world. Usually, private gardens were protected or guarded by a rock wall. This was the picture Solomon painted in the Shulammite's mind. She was a private garden, hidden behind a protective wall.

Notice Solomon didn't compare his beloved to just any garden, but a garden filled with a variety of fruits, spices, and scents: pomegranates, henna, nard, saffron, calamus, cinnamon, myrrh, aloes, every kind of incense tree, and the finest spices. He took great pleasure in gazing at his bride's beautiful landscape as well as grazing on the choice fruits of her body. Biblical scholar Craig Glickman clarified, "Her sensual body and aromatic fragrances are these fruits with mythical power. So when Solomon describes additional details of her garden paradise, he sensitively crafts poetic compliments of her intimate sexuality."[12]

The ESV and NASB translate verse 13 as "your shoots are an orchard of pomegranates." The NLT reads, "Your thighs shelter a paradise of pomegranates with rare spices." Most likely what Solomon was referring to were the delicacies that lay between her thighs.

Let me stop here and take a deep breath. Some of this is hard for me to write. It might be difficult for you to read. Blush alert. Pastor J. D. Greear said, "Solomon [is] speaking under the inspiration of the Holy Spirit, and here's what you need to get your mind around . . . God is into a level of sensuality that most of us are not even comfortable talking about. You see, we have thought about God as the enemy of sexual pleasure, and these passages assure us that not only is he not against it, he is the Creator of sexual pleasure."[13]

So let's keep going. Solomon does.

The Shulammite's virginity had been like a locked-up garden, an enclosed spring, a sealed fountain. And now, on her wedding night, she was giving her husband the key—the only man who would ever have access. As Levi Lusko said, "Solomon praised his bride . . . as a garden enclosed—closed off to trespassers and open only to him (4:12). He belonged to a club so exclusive that it only had one member."[14]

I remember one morning when I sat alone on a dock overlooking the marshes of Topsail Island, North Carolina. Herons flew overhead. Sea oats waved in the early morning breeze. Calm waters mirrored the wispy sky. I tried to imagine the early explorers as they came upon that beautiful island for the very first time. Awe and wonder settled on my ponderings. I think that's what Solomon felt as he gazed upon his wife's body for the first time. He was the great explorer. She the magnificent discovery.

Responding with Delight

How did the bride respond to her husband's loving advances? With passionate sensual ecstasy! In Song of Songs 2:7 and 3:5, she begged her friends not to awaken love until the right time. Now was the right time. She was ready to awaken love with God's blessing.

> Awake, north wind,
>   and come, south wind!
> Blow on my garden,
>   that its fragrance may spread everywhere.
> Let my beloved come into his garden
>   and taste its choice fruits. (4:16)

When the Shulammite spoke of the north and south winds, they were pretty much what you'd guess. She had come to a climax of ecstasy. The north winds were strong and the south winds were gentle. She was ready to love her husband with everything she had, holding nothing back. This is every husband's dream. He longs for his wife to want him sexually. He wants her to be responsive to his touch, receptive to his advances, and released to enjoy him fully as he enjoys her.

At this point, Solomon and his wife had become what God had fashioned a married couple to be: one flesh. C. S. Lewis, in his book *Mere Christianity*, described the "one flesh" unity of marriage in such a beautiful way:

> The Christian idea of marriage is based on Christ's words that a man and wife are to be regarded as a single organism—for that is what the words "one flesh" would be in modern English. And the Christians believe that when He said this He was not expressing a sentiment but stating a fact—just as one is stating a fact when one says that a lock and its key are one mechanism, or that a violin and a bow are one musical instrument. The inventor of the human machine was telling us that its two halves, the male and the female, were made to be combined.[15]

When the Shulammite responded to her husband, she made sure that he knew what was previously "her garden" was now "his garden." She was fully his, just as he was fully hers.

What a stunning picture as we end chapter 4, with the bride handing the key to her husband and his unlatching the lock. What began in the garden of Eden with the first man and woman continued with Solomon and his bride as she lovingly gave her garden to him.

Savoring the Holy Gift

My maternal grandmother had twelve children. My paternal grandmother *only* had six (which I say tongue in cheek). They were both farm girls back in the early 1900s. I'm sure birth control never crossed their minds. When I was a teenager, I asked my paternal grandmother how she prevented getting pregnant back in the day. Horrified, she turned to me and replied, "I just didn't do the evil thing!"

I laughed. She didn't.

No disrespect to my grandmother, but if anyone says that sex is dirty or shameful, we have an entire Bible to contradict them. God created the gift of sex for a husband and wife to enjoy in the safety of marriage and called it good (Genesis 1:31). We are to "honor marriage, and guard the sacredness of sexual intimacy between wife and husband" (Hebrews 13:4 THE MESSAGE). To honor something means that you put a high value on it; you esteem it as valuable. Sex within marriage is a good thing; it's a God thing.

We are not "less holy" when we are passionately loving our husbands, and we should never be embarrassed or feel guilty about it. I honestly think the Enemy who comes to "steal and kill and destroy" (John 10:10) has done a pretty good job of distorting what intimacy should be between a husband and a wife. Let's not let him win.

> Sex within marriage is a good thing; it's a God thing.

It is easy to think of a *marriage* as a holy union designed by God. But we must remember that *sex* is also a holy union designed by God. The oneness that occurs in physical intimacy is not matched in any other way. If you strip away the spiritual and emotional significance of sex, it becomes a physical source of pleasure that lasts for a moment. When you grasp the God-intended dimension of the physical union, it becomes a renewal of the marriage covenant that lasts for a lifetime. "There's more to sex than mere skin on skin. Sex is as much spiritual mystery as physical fact" (1 Corinthians 6:16 THE MESSAGE).

Matt Chandler said, "There was something *holy* taking place between husband and wife [in Song of Songs 4]. It was sacred, special, unique. 'Holy' has often been defined as 'being set apart for special use.' Sex certainly fits that description. It is not for everybody. It is set aside for special use in marriage. Sex is holy."[16]

When you consider physical intimacy from God's perspective, rather than the current culture's perception, you begin to comprehend the depth and breadth—the weightiness and incredible value—of the gift.

Glowing in the Aftermath

Solomon understood the gift and the Giver—and he was thankful for both. Song of Songs 5:1 really seems like it should be attached to the end of chapter 4. The couple had made love for the first time, and Solomon was glowing in the aftermath.

> I have come into my garden, my sister, my bride;
> I have gathered my myrrh with my spice.
> I have eaten my honeycomb and my honey;
> I have drunk my wine and my milk. (Song 5:1)

Solomon reveled and rested in the release of passion. The months of dreaming about being joined as man and wife had finally ended; it was now their reality. He seemed euphoric as he remembered their night of lovemaking. The once tense muscles relaxed. The tension of restraint was released. The buildup of hormonal urges subsided. Like exhausted dancers at the end of a raucous song, the couple rested. There was no guilt or shame but pure joy in knowing the night was sanctioned and sanctified by God. The union of their bodies was complete; the journey of their souls intertwining had taken a monumental leap forward.

Remember, as strange as it may seem to us, there was a party going on outside the bedchamber. We aren't really sure who said the next words: "Eat, friends, and drink; drink your fill of love" (v. 1). Some say it was Solomon calling through the door for the party to carry on without him; he was going to be awhile. Others think it could be God's voice encouraging the couple to enjoy the gift he had given.

"Drink up!" the Creator shouted. "This is a gift I have given to you! Enjoy!"

Either way, the Bible makes it clear that sexual intimacy between a husband and wife is something to celebrate. At this midway mark of the love song, all was right with their world.

But we know what they didn't know quite yet. Marriage isn't one long honeymoon. If someone tells you it is, don't believe a word of it. Life is hard. Marriage is hard. Weaving throughout the most passionate lifelong love affairs are threads of disappointment, disillusionment, and discord. The question is, how will we handle the discord when it comes? How would they? It all starts with grace.

Chapter 6

Trouble in Paradise

"What do you think happened?" my husband asked our friend. "What was the root cause of your divorce?"

"It wasn't just one thing," Brent replied. "We both made mistakes. A culmination of criticism and lack of respect chipped away at the very foundation until there was nothing left to stand on. I tried my best to please her, but nothing I ever did was good enough. I couldn't even load the dishwasher to suit her. She huffed and puffed that I didn't help around the house more. When I did, I never did it well enough. Who wants even to try when he or she is criticized for doing it?

"On top of that, we very rarely had sex. I'm guessing two or three times a year on a good year. Even then I could tell she wasn't interested. It was more like she was doing me a favor, which wasn't a favor at all. It made me feel less loved after it was over. Honestly, her words were so disrespectful and caustic; I didn't really desire her sexually anyway. By the time we separated, we hadn't had sex in more than a year."

Now, girlfriend, we both know that there are always two sides to every story. I'm sure this man's ex-wife had her own list of valid complaints. As Dr. Phil says, "No matter how flat you make a pancake, it still has two sides." (Regardless of what you think about Dr. Phil, you've got to admit that is a great statement.) Yes, the woman may be able to point to other major hurdles in the marriage, but I want us to see the problem from a man's perspective. In the cauldron of disrespect, dissatisfaction, and disappointment brewed a dwindling of desire for sexual intimacy from both parties.

I'm sure the possibility of waning passion never entered Solomon's nor the Shulammite's mind on their wedding night. It certainly never entered mine. I wonder if you had the same thought I had on my honeymoon: *We're going to be different from other couples. We're going to be like we are on our honeymoon forever. I can't even imagine going one day without hugging and kissing my man.*

Nice thought. Then real life begins. Passion is still possible, but not without being intentional and mindful. The infection of indifference toward intimacy is one of those little foxes that can sneak in and destroy a marriage before you even notice the pesky critter is in the garden.

Even Solomon and the Shulammite's marriage was not immune to the invasive infection of indifference. I'm sure it surprised Solomon just as much as reading about it surprised me.

The Locked-Up Garden

Song of Solomon 4 ended with a beautiful picture of passionate love-making and the afterglow of requited desire. The Shulammite had given her husband the key to her locked-up garden, and he had entered to enjoy all the fruits saved just for him. But in chapter 5 it seems something went awry. The Shulammite's door was slammed shut, and Solomon couldn't find the key. Let's join her in the bedroom as he came knocking.

> I slept but my heart was awake.
> Listen! My beloved is knocking:
> "Open to me, my sister, my darling,
> my dove, my flawless one.
> My head is drenched with dew,
> my hair with the dampness of the night."

I have taken off my robe—
must I put it on again?
I have washed my feet—
must I soil them again? (Song 5:2–3)

"Open to me, my sister, my darling, my dove, my flawless one." Can't you just hear his wooing through the paneled door? He's cooing the fourfold words of adoration, words that at one time made her heart melt like butter on a hot biscuit. The man is smooth. He can't wait to see his woman. To be with her. To make love to her. But she's not interested.

"Not now, honey," she says. "I'm tired. I've already washed my face, brushed my teeth, and put on my pj's. Besides, I'm halfway asleep already." (That's a modern-day translation—not that I would know.)

We've all been there. Go ahead. Admit it.

Before the Shulammite and Solomon were married, she couldn't wait to hop in bed with her man. She thought about it all the time and dreamed about it every night. She had to have talks with herself to wait until the honeymoon. And now that she had him, she wasn't all the interested. She was taking him for granted and turning him away, apathetic toward the man who had once made her "faint with love" (2:5). The Shulammite still called Solomon her *dodi* (5:2, 4–6, 8), but she sure didn't treat him like one.

Author Stu Weber reminds us, "A woman can so *easily* crush a man's spirit. With a look. With a word. With a shrug of indifference. . . . On the other hand, a woman is equally capable of causing her husband's spirit to soar."[1] When the Shulammite heard the knock, she had a choice: crush his spirit or make his heart soar. She chose the former.

It's interesting that in these eight short chapters of romance, marriage, and sexual intimacy, 20 percent of the content is dedicated to conflict. Perhaps the greatest lesson is that these verses are included at all. Yes, there will be ups and downs in marriage. Passion will ebb and flow. It's up to us to recognize when the low tides of intimacy threaten to ground the boat on the sandbar of apathy.

Most conflict and frustration in marriage is a result of unmet expectations. This snapshot of the Shulammite's marriage is no exception. Solomon had been out working all day and hoped to spend some "quality time" with his wife. He was expectant. It could be that she expected him to come home from work at a certain time and then got frustrated when he didn't. She was expectant. Or perhaps she expected him to communicate more clearly about his plans and was disappointed when he kept her guessing. We certainly see that he expected her to be glad to see him, and she wasn't. Whatever the case, unmet expectations were the breeding ground for their first recorded conflict as a married couple.

The issue of unmet expectations is almost always tied to self-centeredness, one of the main enemies of marriage. If self-gratification and personal satisfaction are on the throne of a marriage, it will not be a happy kingdom. It is only through the power of the Holy Spirit working in us and through us that we can truly put our selfish desires aside for the desires of another. As Tim Keller wrote, "The work of the Spirit makes Christ's saving work real to our hearts, giving us supernatural help against the main enemy of marriage: sinful self-centeredness."[2] Often, when a wife is caught up in how her husband is not meeting her needs, or the husband is focused on how the wife is not meeting his, arguments become about what is best for the individual rather than what is best for the marriage. However, if we focus on what is best for the marriage, self has to be knocked off the throne. That *is* Jesus' seat after all.

> It's up to us to recognize when the low tides of intimacy threaten to ground the boat on the sandbar of apathy.

I could say a lot about the importance of learning how to resolve marital conflict in a healthy fashion. Bookstore shelves sag with volumes of how to fight fair, settle disagreements, and tackle problems without attacking the person. Important books. Powerful lessons. However, in these pages, we're going to follow Solomon and the Shulammite's lead and focus on one particular conflict—one little fox that crept into their relationship. This scene isn't about just any conflict. It is a conflict of sexual apathy and rejection.

He knocked . . . she didn't answer.

The Danger of Indifference

Marriages typically go through three stages. The first stage is the romantic or the honeymoon stage. The word *honeymoon* literally means "sweet month," but hopefully the honeymoon stage lasts longer than a month. One study suggests that the honeymoon stage typically lasts two years, six months, and twenty-five days.[3] That's pretty specific. I wouldn't go checking your calendar and marking off the days. Whatever the length, the honeymoon stage is a sweet season of romance and passion with little conflict. The couple is getting to know each other and still believes that Prince Charming has indeed married Cinderella.

The next stage is often called the disillusionment or distraction phase. The couple becomes distracted with life: taking care of a home, raising a family, building a career, and managing finances. They may become disillusioned about what they thought their marriage would be like. At times Prince Charming acts more like the warty frog and Cinderella like the evil stepmother. The rose-colored glasses come off and reality sets in. The couple realizes it takes work to keep a marriage strong. This is where many marriages fall back to earth with a thud.

The final stage is dissolution, resignation, or contentment and commitment. Forty percent of married couples dissolve their marriages in this phase. They give up and say it's just not worth the trouble. Some resign themselves to having a mediocre marriage with little expectation of true happiness. And then there are those who decide to work on their relationship and commit to love their mate fully and biblically for the rest of their lives. These are the happy ones. Since you're holding this book, I'm thinking that's you.

In Song of Solomon 5, the couple was moving into the second phase. The honeymoon was over, and real life came knocking at the door.

Back in those days it was common for the king and queen to have separate bedrooms. That would explain why Solomon knocked on the Shulammite's chamber door in the middle of the night. The dew-drenched husband came to his wife's bedroom, anxious to be with her and perhaps make love to her. Maybe he had been dreaming about her all day. Perhaps the scent of myrrh reminded him of that sachet between her breasts. It could be that he had been out in the fields and couldn't wait to get back to her and simply talk over his day and snuggle. But when he got to her room, that garden was locked up for the evening.

Have you ever ignored the knock? Have you ever dismissed your husband's desire or rejected his advances? Have you ever left your man figuratively standing out in the cold? I'll admit that I have, and I never feel quite settled in the silence that follows or sleep very well in the stillness.

Let's look at what Paul wrote to the Corinthians about the dangers of withholding sex in a marriage: "The husband should fulfill his marital duty to his wife, and likewise the wife to her husband. The wife does not have authority over her own body but yields it to her husband. In the same way, the husband does not have authority over his own body but yields it to his wife. Do not deprive each other except perhaps by mutual consent and for a time, so that you may devote yourselves to prayer. Then come together again so that Satan will not tempt you because of your lack of self-control" (1 Corinthians 7:3–5).

What Paul was saying is this: Wives must put their husbands' needs above their own. Husbands must put their wives' needs above their own. Tommy Nelson wrote, "Each must give sacrificially and generously to the other, in sexual behavior and in all other ways in a marriage. Marriage is mostly about giving, not receiving. Only the holy and selfless can truly be great lovers."[4]

Now let's look at that same passage from 1 Corinthians taken from Eugene Peterson's paraphrase, *The Message*:

> It's good for a man to have a wife, and for a woman to have a husband. Sexual drives are strong, but marriage is strong enough to contain them and provide for a balanced and fulfilling sexual life in a world of sexual disorder. *The marriage bed must be a place of mutuality*—the husband seeking to satisfy his wife, the wife seeking to satisfy her husband. Marriage is not a place to "stand up for your rights." Marriage is a decision to serve the other, whether in bed or out. Abstaining from sex is permissible for a period of time if you both agree to it, and if it's for the purposes of prayer and fasting—but only for such times. Then come back together again. Satan has an ingenious way of tempting us when we least expect it. I'm not, understand, commanding these periods of abstinence—only providing my best counsel if you should choose them. (emphasis added)

The marriage bed should be a place of mutuality—the husband seeking to satisfy his wife, the wife seeking to satisfy her husband. Time and time again the Bible points to mutual responsibility to serve each other in marriage. Even in the often-debated passage about submission in Ephesians 5:21–33, Paul led with the words, "Submit to one another out of reverence for Christ."

Notice in the letter to the Corinthians that Paul didn't imply that it was only the husband who had sexual needs. He was assuming that the wife had needs and desires as well. Some have said that the Bible is oppressive toward women, but this passage shows otherwise. In Paul's day women were considered their father's property. When they married, that ownership was passed to the husband for the purpose of producing legitimate heirs who would inherit property and carry on the family name. But Paul's radical teaching put women on the same level with their husbands when it came to sexual intimacy and marital rights. Paul redefined marriage as a context for mutual satisfaction, a call to serve each other in every way.

Paul was assuming that couples were having sex and having sex regularly. In fact, he encouraged it! In his estimation the only time a couple should abstain from sexual intimacy is by mutual consent or agreement, for a time of prayer and fasting. But ask any married person who is not having sex the reason why, and I can almost guarantee it's not because they are in an extended time of prayer and fasting. Discounting illness or injury, most of the time lack of sex for an extended period of time is due to bitter resentment or self-centered apathy. However, other factors such as pornography, self-stimulation, verbal abuse, alcoholism, obesity, childhood trauma, painful intercourse, and certain medications can decrease libido and sex drive. Whether it is current sin, past experiences, or medical issues, the lack of intimacy in marriage needs to be addressed. No one should ever be embarrassed to talk to a professional if these types of issues are causing intimacy problems. That's what they are there for.

Perhaps one of the most important things *we* can do to protect intimacy for a lifetime is to guard against apathy or indifference. We can also root out bitterness due to unmet expectations and relinquish resentment due to disappointment. However, I don't believe we can do either in our own strength. It is only through the power of God working in us and through us that we are able to control our emotions or the actions that follow. Prayer and practice are two keys to experiencing life to the fullest and marriage at its best.

Painting an Easy Target on His Back

Let's go back to Paul's letter to the Corinthians for a moment. I'll admit, some of those words cause my hackles to rise. If my husband quoted, "The wife does not have authority over her own body but yields it to her husband" on a night I wasn't particularly feeling romantic, I'd probably knock him upside the head (not really, but it probably wouldn't go well). However, we need to take a closer look at Paul's warning.

What did Paul tell us about the possible repercussions of withholding sex from our spouses? It paints a target of temptation on the back of the one left unfulfilled. The Enemy is an opportunist, and he is looking for just the right time to put temptation in your man's path. The Devil gets just as excited about a marriage without sex as he does about sex without marriage. Both are out of God's will.

Being unfulfilled sexually in a marriage puts out the welcome mat for the Devil to move right in. Yes, we need to pray for our husbands to resist temptation, but we also need to put some action behind those words. James's warning, "Faith without deeds is useless" (2:20), applies to this area of our marriages as well. As one husband said, "Stop praying for me all the time and make love to me instead!"

When you withhold sex from your husband, you are withholding what you covenanted to give him on your wedding day. It is like saying "I will" but then switching it up on him and saying "I won't." If you say, "Well, he doesn't deserve it. He doesn't treat me the way Solomon treated his wife," then you are turning sex into a reward for good behavior. God did not create sex between a husband and wife as a reward for good behavior or a manipulative tool to get what you want. Intimacy is first and foremost a response to God's idea and ideal. When you respond to your husband when you don't think he deserves it, you are mirroring Jesus, who gives us grace when we don't deserve it either. You are choosing to love like Christ. If you want to change your husband, punishment won't do it. Grace and love will. Jesus shows us that.

Sometimes the wife is more interested in sex than the husband. Studies show that at least 20 percent of wives belong to this camp.[5] When it is the wife who is less interested than the husband, sex still usually occurs. When it is the husband who is not interested, it rarely occurs or never occurs. Just as a woman would not want her husband to demand sex, a husband in this situation doesn't want his wife to nag him about it. Threats and complaints usually make matters worse. Again, this is a time for some soul-searching and professional intervention to discover the root cause for his lack of desire. It could be something as simple as low testosterone—an easy fix. Or it could be more complicated with issues a counselor could help unravel.

> The Devil gets just as excited about a marriage without sex as he does about sex without marriage.

Let me interject here that I'm speaking of relatively emotionally healthy couples. Sexual addiction, physical and verbal abuse, and pornography are more complicated and challenging matters. These will destroy a marriage and need to be addressed, most effectively with a professional. But for those of us with the more garden-variety struggles, we need to be on the lookout continually for the little foxes of apathy and indifference that can sneak in and ruin the relationship.

Fulfilling His Greatest Desire

What about those nights when you're just not in the mood? What do you do then? If you move ahead with resentment in your heart—because you feel as if it's your marital "duty" as a wife—your husband will be able to tell. If you have the attitude, "I don't really want to do this, but I'll get through it to satisfy him," guess what? He won't be satisfied at all. Yes, he might feel a release once the song is sung, but he will not be fulfilled.

A husband doesn't want duty; he wants desire. How would I feel if Steve came home on our anniversary, handed me a dozen roses, and said the following: "I bought you these roses, because it's our anniversary. I personally think it's a waste of money, but I know it's my duty to buy you flowers and give you a card. I even underlined a few words. Here they are. Hope you like them." I'd throw those puppies in the trash! And, yet, that's how many wives approach the marriage bed, especially after they've been married a few years. And you know what? The husband of such a wife knows when a wife wants to make love and when a wife is having sex out of duty. Most men would rather reshingle a roof in hundred-degree heat than have sex with a wife who is doing it out of duty. A man is sexually fulfilled when he knows that his wife is also fulfilled. Duty will not get him there.

So what do you do if you don't have the desire, but you also don't want to act out of duty? There is another choice. Act out of a decision to love. This is the opposite of duty because of the heart behind the action.

Duty is an attitude of obligation that says, "I don't want to do this, but I feel like I have to." A decision to love says, "I'm not in the mood, but I am deciding to put my husband's desires above my desires in order to love him selflessly."

In her book *For Women Only*, Shaunti Feldhahn shared the results of a professional survey about what men are thinking and feeling.

> On each survey and in my random interviews around the country, an urgent theme emerged: Men want more sex than they are getting. And what's more, they believe that the women who love them don't seem to realize that this is a crisis—not only for the man, but for the relationship. . . . For your husband, sex is more than just a physical need. Lack of sex is as emotionally serious to him as, say,

> his sudden silence would be to you, were he simply to stop communicating with you. It is just as wounding to him, just as much a legitimate grievance—and just as dangerous to your marriage.[6]

She goes on to say,

> In a very deep way, your man often feels isolated and burdened by secret feelings of inadequacy. Making love with you assures him that you find him desirable, salves a deep sense of loneliness, and gives him the strength and well-being necessary to face the world with confidence. And, of course, sex also makes him feel loved—in fact, he can't feel completely loved without it.[7]

In Shaunti's survey of married men, 97 percent "said getting enough sex wasn't, by itself, enough—they wanted to feel wanted."[8] Three-fourths said they "would still feel empty if their wives weren't both engaged and satisfied."[9]

"Not tonight, dear" says to a man that he is not capable of turning on his wife. It tells him that she cares more about her sleep than loving him. Now, that probably isn't what she means at all. Most likely she's physically tired, mentally worn out, or emotionally drained. But that's not how he interprets it, mainly because he can still want to have sex when he is physically tired, mentally worn out, or emotionally drained. For him, sex is the magic cure. A husband's self-image is vitally linked to his sexuality, so when a wife resists his advances, he sees it as a personal rejection. This tears at the heart of his self-esteem. If he knows his wife wants him, then he feels his world is a safe place.

George Gilder wrote in *Men and Marriage*, "The truth is, the typical man worries a lot. He worries about his sexual performance, his wife's enjoyment, and his ability to satisfy her. A man who feels like a failure in the marriage bed will seldom have the deep, abiding self-respect for which he longs."[10]

That seems contrary to popular belief, doesn't it? Modern men are portrayed via the media as always being confident and assertive sexually. But most are not as confident as they might seem. Did you know that almost every time your husband initiates intimacy, he has an inkling of fear that you'll turn him down? He's making himself vulnerable to rejection time and time again. But, as Jill Renich writes, "To receive him with joy, and to share sexual pleasure builds into him a sense of being worthy, desirable and acceptable." To please your husband sexually is to build his sense of value as a man.[11]

Here's another way to look at it. We can view sexual intimacy as something we *have* to do or something we *get* to do. This principle of perspective holds true with many areas of life. A woman who has experienced years of infertility doesn't think, "I have to bathe this child." She gratefully thinks, "I get to bathe this child." When an unemployed man finally lands a job, he doesn't say, "I have to go to work." He says, "I get to go to work." The spirit of obligation is the enemy of joy. So which will it be? Obligation or opportunity? Have to or get to? We get to choose.

Most likely neither you nor I will want to say yes every time our husbands make a move. If you do truly need to wait until a better time, though, make sure that your words are tender and kind. Make sure he knows, without a shadow of a doubt, that you are crazy in love with him—that you're not rejecting him.

I don't know about you, but sometimes, when I am not particularly in the mood but am determined to serve and love my husband well, all it takes to help me get there is my intentional welcoming of his advances. Here's the great thing about how God made husbands and wives to respond to each other: after a few minutes of caressing, I *am* in the mood! Oxytocin and dopamine start to flow to the brain, and *bam*—my attitude is miraculously transformed. Isn't God brilliant? When our hearts are right, God ignites the fire, and it's a win-win for both.

Here's an idea: If you *are* too tired, how about saying, "Honey, I am so tired tonight. But if you can wait until tomorrow, I promise I'll make it worth the wait"? Then prepare your mind, follow through, and make him feel like the luckiest man on earth. And don't be surprised if he comes home from work early that day. I suggest the twenty-four-hour rule. If you say no to your husband, then make sure you say yes within twenty-four hours. Don't let too much time pass. It becomes an elephant in the bedroom, which weighs heavily on the heart.

The spirit of obligation is the enemy of joy.

I hope this chapter doesn't make you feel guilty for a lack of interest in meeting your husband's sexual needs or angry that he is wired the way he is. Remember, God made him that way. My hope is that you'll understand the emotional link to intimacy that the warrior in him may not easily reveal. I hope that you'll understand how his confidence and security is bound up in his wife's response to him physically. God has given wives incredible power to build up or tear down their husbands. I pray we will use it well.

Extending Forgiveness and Grace

I'm sure that Solomon was disappointed when his Shulammite didn't open the door and respond to his sweet words. Any man would have been. She basically told him to go sleep on the couch . . . his couch. As he stood outside in the night air, he most likely felt unloved and unwanted. Here's what happened next:

> My beloved thrust his hand through the latch-opening;
> my heart began to pound for him.
> I arose to open for my beloved,
> and my hands dripped with myrrh,

my fingers with flowing myrrh,
        on the handles of the bolt.
I opened for my beloved,
        but my beloved had left; he was gone. (Song 5:4–6)

Solomon didn't respond as you or I might expect. He didn't get angry or bang on the door to demand entrance. He didn't yell or scream in frustration. He could have said, "Hey, I'm the king. How dare you ignore me! I rescued you from working in the fields all day. Look how I've provided for you! And this is the thanks I get?" Instead, he simply slipped his hand through the keyhole and poured myrrh on the latch. In other words, he left his calling card.

The keyholes in Solomon's day were large enough to put your hand through. The bottom had a ledge. That's where Solomon left his gift. All through the Song, the couple referred to myrrh as their special perfume. Perhaps you have a special perfume that your husband loves. Maybe he has a certain cologne that drives you wild. Myrrh was their fragrance.

Rather than stomp away angrily, Solomon poured their special perfume on the latch to let the Shulammite know he had been there. When she put her hand on the lever to open the door, her hand became drenched in the love he left for her.

Solomon's response did not mirror his wife's rejection. Paul wrote, "Make sure that nobody pays back wrong for wrong, but always strive to do what is good for each other and for everyone else" (1 Thessalonians 5:15). We tend to read verses such as these and think of everyone other than our spouses, but there's no one more important to apply this verse to than the one we call ours.

As husbands and wives, we are going to hurt each other. We are going to make each other angry—furious, as a matter of fact. Learning how to respond to difficult situations is an important key to lifelong intimacy. As I mentioned earlier, there are many effective tools available to learn how to fight fair. I do suggest you read the books and practice the principles. The bottom line, though, is that our motives, attitudes, and hoped-for outcomes must be examined as we act and react to each other. Angry outbursts or passive-aggressive withdrawals are equally destructive to a healthy relationship. Solomon did neither but left a "note" to let her know that he still loved her. He extended grace and forgiveness before she even asked.

I know this example is of a husband's loving response to his wife's unloving action; however, we women can learn so much from Solomon. What a wonderful example of how we can respond with kindness when what we'd really like to do is throw a hissy fit and make our husbands pay for how they've hurt us. Solomon later wrote, "A gentle answer turns away wrath, but a harsh word stirs up anger" (Proverbs 15:1). His gentle answer melted his bride's heart. Oh, that we wives would do the same.

But, by the time the Shulammite opened the door, her man was gone. She could have said, "Fine. I don't care. Go off and pout then." She could have climbed back in bed and gone right back to sleep. But she didn't. She tore off after him in a panic.

> I opened for my beloved,
>   but my beloved had left; he was gone.
>   My heart sank at his departure.
> I looked for him but did not find him.
>   I called him but he did not answer.
> The watchmen found me
>   as they made their rounds in the city.
> They beat me, they bruised me;
>   they took away my cloak,
>   those watchmen of the walls!
> Daughters of Jerusalem, I charge you—
>   if you find my beloved,
> what will you tell him?
>   Tell him I am faint with love. (Song 5:6–8)

This scenario sounds much like her dream in chapter 3 but with a greater sense of urgency. You can almost feel the panic as if she were saying, "What have I done? What have I done?" Rather than sit in her room and wait for him to come back to her, she went looking for him, seeking reconciliation as soon as possible.

As we saw in Song of Solomon 3, the night watchmen were guards that patrolled the city walls. They would have known she was the queen, and I doubt they would have laid a hand on her. I suspect she was using poetic imagery. Every time she asked someone if he or she had seen her man and they replied that they hadn't, she felt beat up and bruised by her own actions. Either way, whether literal or figurative, her heart took a beating. She showed us just how dangerous apathy in marriage can be.

I suspect Solomon's kindness toward her in leaving the calling card of myrrh on the door latch exacerbated her feelings of remorse. Sometimes it almost feels better when someone yells back at you than when they kill you with kindness. Paul called that heaping "burning coals" on someone's head (Romans 12:20). When our bad attitude is met with love, there's an ache of remorse, a wishing we could take it all back.

As Rob Flood wrote, "The course of a conflict is not determined by the person who initiates, but by the person who responds."[12] Whether you are in the wrong or your husband is in the wrong, the person with the power to determine the ending of the story lies with the one who responds. Solomon responded to the Shulammite's refusal with grace and love. She replied with repentance and remorse.

Surrounding Yourself with the Right Kind of Friends

We haven't given much attention to the third set of characters in this song. I think of them as the backup singers. They are referred to in the heading as "friends" (NIV), "others" (ESV), and "daughters of Jerusalem"

(NKJV). I consider them "friends"—my friends. The Shulammite surrounded herself with positive friends who supported her marriage. Never once do we hear them speak disparagingly about Solomon. On the contrary, they encouraged the Shulammite to think the best of her husband and to remember what drew her to him in the first place.

> How is your beloved better than others,
> most beautiful of women?
> How is your beloved better than others,
> that you so charge us? (Song 5:9)

What do your friends tell you when you get in a spat with your man? Do they take your side and tell you what a dog he is? Do they feed your feelings of anger and bitterness with the fuel of resentment? Or do they listen with understanding but ultimately lead you back to restoring the relationship?

Karen was struggling in her marriage and confided in her childhood friend, Brittany. "I wouldn't take that from any man," Brittany said. "He's a dog for treating you that way. I never liked him in the first place. You're too good for him. You deserve someone who appreciates you!"

Karen left their conversation angrier than ever. *Brittany's right,* she thought. *I do deserve better than this. Who does he think he is anyway? I'll show him.*

Brittany's comments added wood to the fire of contention. The truth is, Brittany only knew half of the story. Remember, there are always two sides to that flat pancake. Girls, we don't need friends who tear our husbands down, even if they are agreeing with us at the moment. If your friends speak negatively about your man, you need new friends.

Maybe your mom is your best friend. If so, beware of discussing your marital issues with her. She'll almost always side with her little girl, no matter how old you are. Then, when you and your husband kiss and make up, your mama will still be mad at him.

Here's what we can learn from the Shulammite about the sort of friends we need to have and the kind of friend we need to be. We need friends who will encourage us to reach out to our husbands when we want to pull away. To let go of an offense when we want to hold on to a grudge. To think the best when we tend to think the worst. To listen when we want to lash out. To press on when we want to give up.

When you're angry with your husband, a good friend will listen but also try to steer you toward reconciliation. "Now that I've heard all the things you don't like about your husband, tell me what you do like. Why did you fall in love with him in the first place?" These types of questions can change your perspective and encourage you to stick it out. These are the types of questions the Shulammite's friends asked her.

With that little bit of coaxing, the Shulammite remembered why she fell in love with her man when she was but a tenant working in the fields. When there's trouble in paradise, that's the kind of friend we need.

The Shulammite eventually did find her husband after a night of searching. She knew just where to look.

I'm so glad chapter 5 is included in the Song of Solomon, aren't you? It lets us know that even the most romantic beginnings will have raw-hurt middles. No marriage is immune from the infection of indifference, the arctic-cooling of apathy, or the slippery slope of self-centeredness. Recognizing the symptoms early is the key to a quick recovery. Ignoring the signs is a prescription for disaster. And the cure for most of a marriage's ills? Grace and forgiveness. Is it easy? Never. Is it worth it? Always. I know the Shulammite was thankful for good friends to help her over this bump in the road. My hope is that you and I will have the same kind of friends throughout our journeys.

Chapter 7

This Is My Beloved, This Is My Friend

One day Everett came home and told his wife he wanted to invest in a service station in Houston. She thought it was a bad idea and told him so. "You don't have time for a service station, Everett," Jane warned. "I wouldn't put any money in that."

Despite his wife's objections Everett used their money to make the investment. Sometime months later, he called and gave her the bad news: he had lost the station and their money.

When Everett got home from work, Jane wasn't at the door to greet him as she usually was. *Uh-huh,* Everett thought. *She's pouting because we lost this money.* He called out to her using her pet name, "Baby, where are you?"

"I'll be out in a little bit," she called back.

Uh-huh, she's back there pouting, he thought. *She's trying to figure out how to say she told me so.*

Finally, she came out. Everett noticed a pensive look on her face.

"What's wrong?" he asked.

"I'm figuring something out," she answered.

"What're you figuring, Baby?"

"Well, I figured that you don't smoke, and you don't drink. And if you smoked and drank, you would have lost just as much as you lost in the service station, so six in one hand, half a dozen in the other. Let's forget it."

Pastor E. V. Hill told this story about his wife of thirty-two years at her funeral. When he finished there wasn't a dry eye in the house. He concluded by saying, "I only wish I could have been half as good as the woman I married. Through my wife, the Lord gave me an encourager."

God had given Solomon an encourager in the Shulammite, too, but for a moment, she had simply forgotten what a wonderful man he was. From time to time, we all just need a little reminder.

When the Shulammite opened the door and discovered her man was gone, she panicked. Sometimes we need a little wake-up call when we're taking our marriage for granted. Thankfully she had good friends who coaxed her to remember how blessed she really was. "What makes your husband so special?" they asked. "Let's talk about that!" (Song 5:9). Once she got started talking about her *dodi*, it was difficult for her to stop.

> My beloved is radiant and ruddy,
>   outstanding among ten thousand.
> His head is purest gold;
>   his hair is wavy
>   and black as a raven.
> His eyes are like doves
>   by the water streams,
> washed in milk,
>   mounted like jewels.
> His cheeks are like beds of spice
>   yielding perfume.
> His lips are like lilies
>   dripping with myrrh.
> His arms are rods of gold
>   set with topaz.

His body is like polished ivory
    decorated with lapis lazuli.
His legs are pillars of marble
    set on bases of pure gold.
His appearance is like Lebanon,
    choice as its cedars.
His mouth is sweetness itself;
    he is altogether lovely.
This is my beloved, this is my friend,
    daughters of Jerusalem. (vv. 10–16)

Just as Solomon took an inventory of seven of his bride's stunning features on their wedding night, the Shulammite took inventory of ten of his. In the Bible, the number ten, like seven, is a number for perfection.

She started with his complexion. It was ruddy and radiant, tanned by the sun from tending the flocks. The original Hebrew word actually means "to glow" or "to shine." I love that! He's shiny! He's dazzling!

Just as Solomon compared the Shulammite's hair to the flowing black fleece of goats running down the hillside, she compared his wavy hair to the brilliant black ravens flying in the sky. She compared his head (not hair) to the nobility of gold. He wasn't just the king of Israel; he was the king of her heart.

She went on to describe his seductive eyes set like jewels on his handsome face. His eyes brought her a sense of peace, like a gentle dove. This is the only comparison that they both used for each other. They saw love reflected in each other's eyes.

She pondered his yummy cheeks that begged to be kissed, his sensuous lips that dripped with myrrh, and his muscular body that outshone ten thousand men.

Even though he was gentle and tender with her, she admired his strength. She compared his arms to rods of gold set with topaz, certain parts of his body to polished ivory tusks decorated with lapis, and his legs to pillars of marble set on bases of pure gold—all the finest resources that the land had to offer. His stature was like that of the cedars of Lebanon. He stood firm and could not be shaken by the winds of adversity. When she called his mouth "sweetness itself," she most likely was referring to the words he spoke to her—tender, loving, kind. I envision her wanting to hold his face in her hands and give him that kiss he wanted earlier.

"This is my beloved, this is my friend, daughters of Jerusalem," she sighs. "Thank you for reminding me."

Have you forgotten what drew you to your man in the first place? Tomorrow, look at him. Really look at him. Notice his hands. His eyes. His arms. Look at him, and admire his wonderful qualities rather than focusing on his worst.

I wonder what your husband would do if you wrote out your own version of the Shulammite's appraisal of her man. It might be fun to give it a try. Consider writing such a list and giving it to him. Better yet, read it to him and touch each part of his body as you describe what you admire about it.

When it comes to appreciating our husbands, sometimes we just need a little reminder.

Susan attended a class on marriage. Part of the assignment for one of the weeks was to tell her husband something she admired about him. In all their years together, she had never put her admiration into words. It was a big step for her. She didn't quite know how to start, even though she loved her husband. That evening, while he was reading the paper, she sat down next to him on the sofa and began stroking his arm. After a bit, she stopped at the bicep and squeezed. He subconsciously flexed his muscle, and she said, "Oh, I never knew you were so muscular!" He put down the paper, looked at her, and inquired, "What else?" He was so starved for admiration, he invited her to say more.

How about your man? When was the last time you told him that you loved his smile or admired his talent? Can't remember? Well, today could be the day! That's your homework. Use your words to build up that man of yours.

Robert Louis Stevenson said, "Make the most of the best and the least of the worst." Too many times we flip what Stevenson said and make the most of the worst and least of the best. Let's change that. Today. Right now.

What was the Shulammite's final answer to her friends' question? "This is my beloved, this is my friend" (v. 16). When we focus on the positives, we'll most likely come to the same conclusion.

The Power of a Good Word

Other than God's Word, your words are the most powerful words in your husband's life. You have the ability to build him up or tear him down, give him courage or take away his confidence, inspire him to reach for his goals or conspire with his deepest insecurities to make him quit. Let me share another story that E. V. Hill told about how his wife, Jane, used her words to build him up when it would have been so easy to tear him down. You might want to grab a tissue.

One day, when Everett came home after a long, tiresome day at work, he was surprised to see candles lit throughout the house. The kitchen table was set for two and danced with candlelight in their modest home. In his gregarious teasing fashion, Everett turned to his wife and said, "What meanest thou this?"

"Well, we've been married exactly six months today," Jane explained, "and I thought we would eat by candlelight tonight."

That sounded like a welcomed romantic idea to Everett, so he went to the bathroom to wash up for dinner. Jane hadn't put a candle in the bathroom, so Everett turned to flip the switch. No light came on. Then he walked across the hall to the dark bedroom and flipped the switch. No light came on.

Everett went back out to the kitchen, looked Jane in the eyes, and said, "Baby, did they cut the lights off?" And she began to cry.

"You work so hard," she said, "and we're trying so hard. I didn't have quite enough money to pay the light bill, and I didn't want you to know about it. So I thought we would just eat by candlelight tonight."

Every time I read Pastor Hill's words about his Jane, I cry. Not because I am sad for his loss, but because I want to be that kind of woman—that kind of wife. I want to be a wife who uses her words to build up her husband rather than tearing him down, who encourages him to reach for his dreams rather than throwing cold water on his enthusiasm, who lets him know that he is loved rather than leaving him questioning his worth.

Upon reflection, Pastor Hill said this about the night the lights went out: "She could have broken my spirit. She could have ruined me. She could have demoralized me. But she said, 'Let's eat by candles. We'll turn the lights on one day. Somehow we'll get these light on. But tonight let's eat by candlelight.'"

Pastor Hill's wife knew something that I want to always remember. A wife has the power to bolster her husband's confidence or break his spirit with but a word. Jane chose to be "his encourager." After the Shulammite came to her senses, she made the same choice.

Proverbs 12:25 reminds us, "Anxiety in a man's heart weighs him down, but a good word makes him glad" (ESV). All through the day your husband has words thrown at him that could cause anxiety to rise and self-esteem to fall. But you, dear one, have the ability to make him glad with a word—and especially glad that he came home to you.

And here's more good news: notice the proverb is about a good *word*. You don't have to have a lot of words. You don't have to wax eloquent, write a discourse, or make a speech. Just one little word can make all the difference. I'm not all that great at one word, but I can certainly do less than ten.

"I'm so proud of you."

"I missed you today."

"I love you so much."

"Thank you for working so hard."

"I'm so glad I married you."

When my friend Pamela's husband calls her, she always answers the phone by saying, "Hey, good-looking!" When I asked her why she did that, she said, "I want him to know he will always be my love and my hero."

I asked her hubby how it made him feel to hear his wife say those words when he called. "It makes me feel like I can do anything!" he replied. "It puts a smile on my face every time." And she has been doing that for more than forty-five years. Two little words. A lifetime of rewards.

> A wife has the power to bolster her husband's confidence or break his spirit with but a word.

When the Shulammite enumerated her husband's magnificent qualities, she did so in front of an audience. "This is my beloved, this is my friend, *daughters of Jerusalem*" (Song 5:16, emphasis added). Nothing makes a man's heart swell more than his wife bragging on him, except when she brags on him in front of others. The Shulammite inspires us to speak positively about our husbands to other people. Better yet, do it in a place where he can hear it. Then watch him smile.

Don't Allow Time to Tarnish Wonder

When I met my husband, Steve, I thought *he* was "radiant and ruddy, outstanding among ten thousand" (v. 10). He loved Jesus and was breathtakingly handsome. Steve was in grad school, which said to me that he was driven, smart, and a hard worker. He drove a twelve-year-old Volkswagen that didn't have air-conditioning or a speedometer. To me, that meant he wasn't materialistic, but thrifty and practical. When the windows of his car fogged up on our first date (because of climate reasons, not long-kissing reasons—honestly), he asked me to reach into the glove box and get out the defroster. When I opened it and discovered an old rag to wipe down the windows, he gave me a big grin. *How clever and witty he is,* I thought. *I just love this man.* On our two-month dating anniversary, Steve brought me two roses and a card that had two tulips on the front. Inside the card the inscription read, "My two lips want to meet your tulips." Ah, yes, he was romantic and witty.

I could go on. I bet you could do the same. These are little gems I tucked away in the treasure chest of memories to pull out from time to time. I encourage you to place memories of the early days of wonder in such a place.

Now, let's jump ahead. A bride walks down the aisle on her wedding day in her princess dress and joins her prince at the altar. The couple says their "I dos" and drives off to live happily ever after. But after the wedding comes the marriage. Hurt feelings. Daily routine. Mounting bills. Pesky in-laws. Whining kids. And who said it was the woman's duty to do the laundry anyway?

After a few years, the couple stops trying to impress each other. He burps and doesn't even try to hide it under his breath. She doesn't take care of her appearance unless she's going out. He leaves the door open when he goes to the bathroom. She cuts down on shaving her legs. He chews with his mouth open. Her sexy nighties turn into flannel. He lives in his sweats. She loves her fuzzy robe and Mickey Mouse bedroom shoes.

His thrifty turns into tightwad. Her fun personality turns into annoying. His adventurous spirit turns into irresponsibility. Her organizational skills turn into a controlling attitude. Now, I know this isn't true across the board. These are huge generalities. But the point is, after a few years of marriage, we can forget why we married that incredible man in the first place. *What was I thinking?* we wonder. *This is not what I signed up for. This is not who I thought he was.* And the truth is, our husbands are probably thinking the same thing.

One way to polish the tarnish of resentment and disappointment off of our original starry-eyed wonder is with words of admiration and appreciation. You can blot out the sun with your thumb if you bring it close enough to your eye. In the same way, you can blot out your husband's admirable qualities if you hold a thumb of disapproval close enough to your heart.

We need to avoid focusing on the 5 percent negative and concentrate on the 95 percent positive. Cheer him on in the good stuff and give the rest to God. I suggest making a list of all your husband's admirable qualities. Not just his outward appearance but also his inner strengths. Keep the list handy and add to it as qualities come to mind. Then, if you're smart, one day you will give him the list.

Sometimes, though, it's not only what we say to our husbands but also what we say to ourselves about our husbands that affect the atmosphere of our homes and our relationships. The term *confirmation bias* refers to the tendency to interpret new evidence as confirmation of one's existing beliefs or theories. It's when people want something to be true, or believe that something is true, and then gravitate toward information that supports their beliefs and reject information that casts doubt on them. Whether you tell yourself that your husband is selfish or selfless, you will begin to look for actions and attitudes to back it up. If you tell yourself your husband is useless around the house, you'll look for evidence to support that and overlook all the ways he does contribute to running the family. If you tell yourself that your husband is a giver, you'll be tuned in to the ways he helps those in his sphere of influence.

You believe more of what you say to yourself than what anyone else says to you. Say positive words about your husband to yourself, and you'll begin to think and act positively toward him. When you are feeling irritated with him, ask yourself, "What have I been telling myself about my husband? Have I been telling myself that he is irresponsible, clueless, lazy, or prideful? Or have I been telling myself that he's a gift from God, a hard worker, a great lover, and a caring friend?" Whatever you tell yourself, you'll believe it.

Once the Shulammite started reminding herself of her husband's positive qualities, she remembered just how blessed she really was. The same will happen in our hearts when we follow her lead.

The Importance of Admiration and Respect

We've already seen that a husband wants to know he is satisfying his wife sexually. But he wants to satisfy her in a host of other ways as well. More than anything, your husband wants to know that you admire and respect him—he wants to be your hero.

Paul taught husbands to love their wives, and wives to respect their husbands (Ephesians 5:33). As much as you long to be loved and cherished, your husband longs to be admired and respected. That's just the way God made him.

What exactly is *respect*? It is a feeling of admiration for someone elicited by his or her abilities, qualities, or achievements. It is holding someone in high regard. We show respect by how we value a man's decisions and abilities. We communicate respect by how we talk to him and about him. If a man doesn't feel respected, he will not feel loved.

You have no control over what happens to your husband in the workplace, but you do have some control over what he feels in the homeplace. His self-esteem teeters on the precipice of your approval, and you can make or break him with your words. If he doesn't feel admiration from you, he will seek other areas where he can succeed. He'll work late at the office to hear "Good job." He'll hang out with the guys on the basketball court to hear "Great shot." He'll go home to Mama to hear "You're such a good boy."

Listen to what a few respondents told me when I surveyed men for my book, *Becoming the Woman of His Dreams*:

> "All men need more encouragement. They need to know that they have at least one big-time fan." —Gene[1]

> "A man dreams of being needed and wanted by a wife. There are times when I know my wife looks up to me, respects me, and honors me. That is when I love her the most and feel the best about myself as well. When I feel strong, I am strong. More than any other person in the world, she holds the key to my confidence." —Al[2]

> "I don't think any single thing takes away a man's strength of character more than the loss of respect. . . . Don't dwell on his weaknesses, but dwell on the positives. Men are in a fight for our lives. We are at war mentally. We're out there trying to conquer the world. A man needs to know that home is a safe place to be instead of feeling like you're leaving one battle for another." —Don[3]

Brenda wrote me about how much her encouraging words meant to her husband. "Every day I make my husband's breakfast and lunch for him to take to work. I always, always put a note of love and affirmation in his lunch bag, just to let him know he is loved, adored, and appreciated. Recently I had some health issues and wasn't able to pack his lunch every day. Today I felt well enough and asked him what he would like for breakfast and lunch. He said, 'Just cook one of those frozen breakfast bowls, and I'll get my own lunch. Oh . . . and my note, don't forget my note. I miss your notes.' My eyes just teared up while typing this," she wrote. "It stopped me in my tracks—something so small meant so much to him."

When God fashioned man and woman in his image, he did something astounding. He gave us the gift of words. He didn't give words to any of the other creatures on the face of the earth. He gave them to you and to me. With our words we can change the course of someone's life. As Scripture tells us, "Death and life are in the power of the tongue" (Proverbs 18:21 NASB). The death and life of a marriage are in the power of the tongue as well.

> You have no control over what happens to your husband in the workplace, but you do have some control over what he feels in the homeplace.

All day long your husband is dealing with people in the workforce with negative words. He needs to know that there is one person who is for him—who is on his side and believes in him. If you could listen to the thoughts in your husband's head, you'd most likely hear whispers of inferiority, insecurity, and inadequacy. Even though most men put on a strong persona, inside they're wondering if they really have what it takes to make it in this world as a man, a provider, a lover, and a friend. Your husband questions his masculinity, his gifts, and his abilities. Let him know he has what it takes to succeed.

William Barclay once said,

> One of the highest of human duties is that of encouragement. . . . It is easy to laugh at people's ideals, to pour cold water on their enthusiasm, to discourage them. The world is full of discouragers; we have a Christian duty to encourage one another. So many times, words of praise or thanks or appreciation or cheer have kept people on their feet. Blessed are those who speak such words.[4]

Men are less likely to expose or admit their need for encouragement than women are, I believe, because it goes against the world's idea of masculinity. Men are taught to be tough and thick-skinned. But they crave admiration and are attracted to sweet words of encouragement like bees are to honey. As Solomon later wrote in Proverbs, "Pleasant words are a honeycomb, sweet to the soul and healing to the bones" (16:24 NASB), but "words of the reckless pierce like swords" (12:18).

Your words become the mirror in which your husband sees himself. In one of his marriage series, Andy Stanley said, "Your husband should be able to tell how much God loves him by the way you treat him—and love him, and admire him. Your husband may have no idea what God is like, but he should be able to know by the way you treat him—by the way you respect him, he will have a glimpse of how much God adores him."[5]

At her friends' prompting, the Shulammite remembered that she was married to the most magnificent man on earth. When she finally found him, I have no doubt she let him know just how she felt.

Every man longs for his woman to do that. They are silently asking, *Do you respect me? Do you admire me? Are you proud of me?* So let's tell them. Let your husband know that he's brave and brilliant, loving and logical, tough and tender, masculine and magnificent, sexy and savvy. That's the stuff of his dreams. Your husband wants not only to *be* loved but also to be *told* that he's loved.

Do you want to see your husband's face light up? Tell him you are amazed that he knows how to ______________, or that you are impressed by his ______________, and then sit back and watch him glow. As the Shulammite said, he'll be shiny.

The Daily Decision to Cheer or Boo

Every day we make decisions to cheer or to boo our men. Think about this. An infant rolls over, and his mama cheers. The five-year-old boy hits the ball off the tee, and his parents cheer. The ten-year-old adolescent crosses the finish line, and his teammates cheer. The high school junior makes a free throw, and the crowd cheers. The college student walks across the stage to receive his diploma, and his family cheers. Then he gets married, and what does he hear?

Mark was a guy who had been cheered on his whole life . . . until he got married. Then all he heard was "boo." Every time Christmas rolled around, he felt as if he was headed for failure. He'd work hard to get Barb the perfect gift, and inevitably it wouldn't be good enough. It wasn't that he didn't like to buy her gifts. He really did. But she never liked them. In twenty-five years he never landed the perfect gift. He knew always to include a gift receipt for easy returns.

Finally, Mark resorted to having Barb tell him exactly what she wanted and where she wanted him to purchase it. On one particular Christmas, Barb made her request. "I want the green bag from Monograms Plus. They have it on display. I want it monogrammed in yellow in a font called Fancy."

Mark felt relieved to know exactly what Barb wanted. *Maybe this time I won't disappoint her and be a failure in the gift-giving department,* he thought.

On Christmas morning Barb opened up her professionally wrapped present. Tears welled up in her eyes. She threw the bag down on the floor, stomped out of the room, and yelled, "You can't do anything right!"

When Mark finally got up the nerve to enter the bedroom, he asked, "What's wrong?"

"You got the wrong bag!" she yelled. "This one looks like a backpack. I wanted the one with the shoulder strap! You don't know me at all! I'd never use something like this. Have you ever seen me with a backpack? You just don't get me!"

Another Christmas. Another disappointment. Another failure. Another boo. "All I ever hear is 'boo,'" he moaned.

The desire to be cheered rather than booed starts at a very early age. We all have it. Your man has it. John Eldredge saw it in his boys.

He had taken his two boys to a place in Colorado Springs called Garden of the Gods. Red sandstone spires look like the backbones of great beasts. Rocky crags. Ragged cliffs. Lots of dirt. A boy's paradise. On this particular day, John and the boys were going rock climbing with all the protective gear. Here's what happened:

> Sam was the first to climb that afternoon, and after he clipped the rope into his harness, he began his attempt.
>
> Things were going well until he hit a bit of an overhang, which even though you're roped in makes you feel exposed and more than a little vulnerable. Sam was unable to get over it and he began to get more and more scared the longer he hung there; tears were soon to follow. So with gentle reassurance I told him to head back down, that we didn't need to climb this rock today, that I knew of another one that might be more fun. "No," he said, "I want to do this." I understood. There comes a time when we simply have to face the challenges in our lives and stop backing down. So I helped him up the overhang with a bit of a boost, and on he went with greater speed and confidence. "Way to go, Sam! You're looking good. That's it . . . now reach up to your right . . . yep, now push off that foothold . . . nice move." . . .
>
> He came to another challenging spot, but this time sailed right over it. A few more moves and he would be at the top. "Way to go, Sam. You're a *wild man*." He finished the climb, and as he walked down from the back side I began to get Blaine clipped in. Ten or fifteen minutes passed, and the story was forgotten to me. But not Sam. While I was coaching his brother up the rock, Sam sort of sidled up to me and in a quiet voice asked, "Dad . . . did you really think I was a wild man up there?"
>
> Miss that moment and you'll miss a boy's heart forever. It's not a question—it's *the* question, the one every boy and man is longing to ask. Do I have what it takes? Am I powerful? Until a man *knows*

> he's a man he will forever be trying to prove he is one, while at the same time shrinking from anything that might reveal he is not. Most men live their lives haunted by the question, or crippled by the answer they've been given."[6]

You, dear wife, have that power, right under your nose, to let the little boy in that grown man's body know that he has what it takes. In his mind he's asking you, *Do you think I'm a wild man?* Let him know that you think he is all that and more!

Strengthening the Bond of Friendship

Remember the love letters from my father-in-law, Bruce, to his bride, Mary Ellen, which I mentioned in chapter 1? As you might expect, each sheet of paper was folded before it was tucked in an envelope. Interestingly, the Song of Solomon is much like a folded letter.

The Song was written using a chiastic structure. A *chiasm* is a repetition of similar ideas in reverse sequence—like taking a piece of paper and folding it down the middle. One half is a mirror image of the other. This organizes the poem into themes and serves to give emphasis to those themes. You'll notice repeated words or phrases as we move along. The second half of the Song is a reflection of the first but goes deeper. In the first half of the letter, the Shulammite mentioned the importance of friendship in a budding romance. In the second half she emphasized the importance of friendship in a deep-rooted relationship and lifelong intimacy.

At the very end of the Shulammite's elaboration of her husband's finest qualities in chapter 5, she took a deep breath and sighed, "This is my beloved, this is my friend" (v. 16). If I were ever going to get a tattoo, this would be it. That's exactly how I feel about my husband. What started as passionate romance with a hint of friendship grew into a deep abiding, an intertwining of souls, a forever friendship—the qualities that tether a couple together for a lifetime.

Solomon first called the Shulammite his friend in chapter 1 (vv. 9, 15). As we've already seen, the Hebrew word *rayah* is translated "darling" in the NIV but literally means "companion."[7] Now the Shulammite says the same about her *dodi*.

Marriage expert John Gottman wrote, "The determining factor in whether wives feel satisfied with the sex, romance, and passion in their marriage is, by 70 percent, the quality of the couple's friendship. For men, the determining factor is, by 70 percent, the quality of the couple's friendship. So men and women come from the same planet after all."[8]

One of the destroyers to lifelong marriage is the slow deterioration of the bond of friendship. Chores. Children. Roles. Responsibilities. Before you know it, lovers are no longer friends sharing an adventurous life but roommates sharing an arduous existence. Sheldon Vanauken called this slow dissolution that catches couples unaware "creeping separateness."

> There is such a thing as creeping separateness. What do young people who are freshly married do? They can't rest when they're apart. They want to be together all the time. But they develop separate interests, especially if they have separate jobs and some separate friends. So they drift apart. Pretty soon they have little in common except, maybe, the children. So the stage is set for one of them to fall in love with someone else. Later they'll say the reason for the divorce was that he/she fell in love with someone else, but it wasn't that at all. It was because they let themselves grow apart.[9]

"We just don't have anything in common."

"We've grown apart."

"He's not the man I married."

"I don't know how this happened."

These are common complaints from couples who have allowed

their friendships to fizzle. A good marriage doesn't just happen. It takes intentionality and creativity to weave commonalities into a life that is intertwined beyond unraveling.

God has placed in each human heart the desire to know and be known. We long for intimacy, even as children. Little girls want a best friend with whom to share secrets, hold hands, and write love notes. Little boys want a blood brother with whom to make a secret pact, have a special handshake, and form a members-only club. While we may have glimpses of intimate friendship throughout our lives, marriage is the pinnacle of true intimacy, or at least it can be.

Oftentimes, this kind of intimacy is difficult to achieve. As with any close friendship, there is the fear "if he really knew me, he may not like me." Intimate friendship goes beyond that fear. A true friend is one who knows all your faults and loves you anyway. Naked and unashamed.

It takes intentionality and creativity to weave commonalities into a life that is intertwined beyond unraveling.

There's no way you are going to share everything with your husband, and you shouldn't. He will have some interests that are solely his, and you will have some interests that are solely yours. I can safely say that with my lack of hand-eye coordination I will never take up golf, and that Steve will never pick up a needle and thread. However, we always make sure to enjoy certain activities together. We have fun! Whether it is dancing the swing at a party, playing Scrabble on a Sunday night, or walking on the beach hand in hand, we play. We share secrets, struggles, and insecurities. We laugh together. Cry together. And do nothing together. He is my lover. He is my friend.

Your spouse should always be your best friend. Oh sure, we need to live in community and have friends of the same gender. But that best friend? That one person in your life with whom you can share your deepest longings and greatest fears? That should be your spouse.

The words we share as friends are one of the most important elements of any marriage. Whether it's encouraging each other to reach for dreams, emboldening each other to stand courageously when weak, romancing each other with words of love, delighting in each other's positive qualities, or sharing as two friends who simply enjoy each other's company. Words are one of the most powerful forces in the universe to strengthen or weaken a marriage, and they're right under your nose.

Chapter 8

Forgiveness and the Dance of Two Camps

My doorbell rang early one cool fall morning. I was surprised to see my disheveled young friend sobbing on my front porch. When I opened the door, she fell into my arms. "My marriage is over!" she wailed. "It's over!"

The good news is that her marriage was not over. She and her husband had just had a humdinger of an argument. He stormed out the door and left for work; she cried for an hour and then made her way to my kitchen table. That evening, they had a long talk, forgave each other, kissed, and made up. That's exactly what Solomon and the Shulammite were about to do in Song of Solomon 6.

I'm so glad the most romantic book in the Bible includes a spat between lovers. It shows us that, even in the best marriages, conflict is inevitable. We'll also see that forgiveness is key to a couple's staying power. As Ruth Graham, the wife of Billy Graham, once said, "A happy marriage is the union of two good forgivers."[1] But when it comes to taking steps toward reconciliation and forgiveness, someone has to make the first move.

We left the Shulammite affectionately enumerating all of her husband's finer qualities at the prodding of her friends. She got so distracted recalling and recounting all the reasons why her husband was the most amazing man on earth that she forgot where she was for a moment. In her dreamy-eyed wonder, it slipped her mind that Mr. Wonderful had knocked on her door and she had refused to let him in—that she had totally ignored his advances and sent him packing. She forgot that she needed to make amends. But thank God for those friends. They reeled her in and roused her back from her mesmerizing stupor.

"Come on, girl. Get back to reality. Remember what you did? Remember what just happened? Don't you think you need to make things right with your man?" First, they prompted her to remember. Then they coaxed her to take action, to make the first move. I just love these friends!

> Where has your beloved gone,
> most beautiful of women?
> Which way did your beloved turn,
> that we may look for him with you? (Song 6:1)

The Shulammite didn't have to wonder where to find her husband. He was consistent in character, conviction, and behavior. She didn't have to speculate if he was gallivanting with another woman, storming around in anger, or planning revenge for her lapse of judgment. That wasn't who he was. Even though they had occasional arguments, misunderstandings, and disappointments as any couple would, she had no doubts about the strength of their relationship or the stability of their commitment. She knew just where to find him.

> My beloved has gone down to his garden,
> to the beds of spices,
> to browse in the gardens
> and to gather lilies.
> I am my beloved's and my beloved is mine;
> he browses among the lilies. (vv. 2–3)

I've read myriad commentaries and books on the Song of Solomon while writing this one, and all of them were written by men. The guys have shared some helpful insights about how men process information. Matt Chandler offered this male perspective on what Solomon was most likely feeling after his wife's rejection:

> He went to the garden. If I had to guess, I think he was probably wrestling with his frustration. He probably knew his frustration wasn't valid. So he sat alone, working through, processing, and praying.
>
> This is a fairly typical male trait. Wives, you may think that in times of conflict, your husband is "shutting down," and this means he's not as engaged, not as invested in the relationship as you. Men tend to process things a little differently than women, though. Women tend to be more verbal in their processing, able to access multiple thoughts and feelings simultaneously and express them fairly quickly. Men need a little more stewing. . . .
>
> Men tend to process more internally. It's likely that Solomon was doing just that. He didn't want to react in a poor way, so he gave her a sign that he loved her and then stole away for a bit to be alone and work through his frustrations.[2]

While that is an interesting report of what goes on in a man's mind, I don't think that's what the Shulammite was describing in 6:2–3. In every other reference to the "garden" or "lilies" in the Song, the couple was referring to physical intimacy. I think she had found her man, and they were making up.

True to the folded letter idea and the repeated themes of a chiasm, the Shulammite's words in 6:3 mirror her words in 2:16–17: "My beloved is mine and I am his; he browses among the lilies. Until the day breaks and the shadows flee." And then there are Solomon's words from chapter 4: "Your breasts are like two fawns, like twin fawns of a gazelle that browse among the lilies" (v. 5). Seven times "lilies"—or in some translations, "lotuses"—refer to the Shulammite's body and one time to Solomon's lips. But every time, "lilies" refers to some aspect of physical intimacy. He gathered and he grazed. Yep, I think they were making up in verses 6:2–3. Her lover was in his garden (4:12, 15–16; 5:1) because she had opened the gate once again.

I love how Solomon welcomed the Shulammite with open arms. Not once do we read that he rebuffed or rebuked her; instead he simply took her in his arms and rekindled their romance. The Shulammite could have pouted for a few days. Solomon could have stewed. But she made the first move toward reconciliation and he reciprocated swiftly. With these selfless attitudes we can never go wrong.

Understanding Biblical Forgiveness

It doesn't take very long for a couple to figure out that marriage isn't a continuously fun and easy ride, a big bundle of happy days tied up with a sparkly bow of hugs and kisses. It's often the sandpaper of chafing personalities, unmet expectations, and hurt feelings that rub us the wrong way and leave us feeling rather raw. Being able to forgive past offenses and let go of past hurts is an essential component for growing a strong marriage and maintaining an intimate relationship that lasts a lifetime.

On the other hand, unforgiveness blocks intimacy on an emotional and physical level. The Gottman Institute, a research-based relationship organization, noted, "The capacity to seek and grant forgiveness is one of the most significant factors contributing to marital satisfaction and a lifetime of love."[3] Without forgiveness, we will never be able to have a healthy, thriving marriage. We can live in the same house, eat the same meals, take the same trips, and raise the same children, but without forgiveness we will live just short of true intimacy of the heart, never quite free to be soul naked and unashamed.

Forgiveness, when we look at it from the Greek perspective with the word *aphiemi,* means "to let go from one's power, possession, to let go free, let escape."[4] Biblical forgiveness means cutting someone loose. This word picture is one in which the unforgiven is roped to the back of the unforgiving. When we refuse to forgive, we bind ourselves to what we hate. When we forgive, we cut the person loose from our backs and set ourselves free as well.

Forgiveness can also be seen in terms of canceling a debt. In the Old Testament, when someone paid a debt, a notice of the debt paid in full was nailed to the lender's door. That is what Jesus did when he was nailed to the cross—our debt was paid in full and nailed to heaven's door. When you forgive your husband, you cancel his debt, which he never could've paid back anyway. Forgiveness is no longer holding the offense against the offender.

I recently received an e-mail from a woman who was still bitter over a statement her husband made to her cousin ten years ago. She and her husband were preparing to celebrate their fiftieth wedding anniversary, and she was dreading it because of his careless words a decade before. She wrote, "Please pray that God mends this title [sic] piece of my heart that has fallen to the ground."

The word *title* was a typo—she meant to type *little.* To me, it was telling. Friend, we can allow our husbands' *little* shortcomings to become the *title* of our story, or we can forgive and write a new storyline. Not only does forgiveness change the title of your story, it changes the ending as well. So, how exactly can we consciously pursue forgiveness?

The first step to forgiveness is prayer. The Bible tells us to pray for our enemies (Matthew 5:44). I hope your husband is never your enemy, but there may be days you feel like he is. So let's follow God's instruction and start by praying for him. It may not turn your husband's hardened heart to putty in your hands, but it will melt the hardness of resentment in your own. I've seen this happen time and time again in my own heart. It's difficult to stay mad at someone when you're praying for him.

How many times are we to forgive? Peter asked Jesus that same question. "Lord, how often should I forgive someone who sins against me? Seven times?"

Jesus answered, "No, not seven times, but seventy times seven" (18:21–22 NLT).

This doesn't mean on the 491st offense we can choose not to forgive. Jesus was saying that there was no limit.

But what about those big offenses? You know the ones I'm talking about. That is a good question. Pornography, alcoholism, drug abuse, and a host of other addictions must be addressed and dealt with for any marriage to survive and thrive. No one is doing his or her spouse any favor by allowing such destructive behavior to continue. To ignore such issues is enabling sin to continue and poisoning the marriage with the arsenic of apathy or fear.

> We can allow our husbands' *little* shortcomings to become the *title* of our story, or we can forgive and write a new storyline.

God's call for us to forgive does not mean that a woman should stay with a man who is abusive or sexually unfaithful. Separation is sometimes the best course of action. The wife needs to make sure that she is safe. A wife can separate from her husband, pray for her marriage, and continue to trust God to bring healing and restoration.

So, yes, there are bigger issues that we do need to address as they come up, sometimes seeking professional help, but this does not mean forgiveness is on hold. There is a difference between forgiveness and trust. This is where the idea of reconciliation gets a bit muddy. Forgiveness can be immediate. Trust is rebuilt through right behavior over a period of time.

In his book *The Purpose Driven Life*, pastor Rick Warren said,

"Forgiveness is letting go of the past. Trust has to do with future behavior. Forgiveness must be immediate, whether or not a person asks for it. Trust must be rebuilt over time. Trust requires a track record. If someone hurts you repeatedly, you are commanded by God to forgive them instantly, but you are not expected to trust them immediately, and you are not expected to continue allowing them to hurt you."[5]

After a betrayal, trust can be built again over time. However, it cannot be built if the one betrayed continues to knock down the blocks of positive behavior with the bat of past offenses.

And what is the ultimate example of forgiveness? The way Jesus forgave you and me. Paul wrote, "Bear with each other and forgive one another if any of you has a grievance against someone. Forgive as the Lord forgave you" (Colossians 3:13). And how did he forgive us? Totally and completely as soon as we asked (1 John 1:9).

Relinquishing Your Rights

I think one of the most difficult aspects of forgiveness is the lingering desire to be right when wronged. We can hang on to our hurts and almost make an idol of them. The offense becomes more important than the repentant offender. We can put the hurt in a prominent place in our hearts, dusting it off every now and then with a rag of resentment, when what we really need to do is throw it in the trash. And that's exactly what Solomon and the Shulammite did.

The Shulammite reached out to her husband for forgiveness and reconciliation. He pulled her in with mercy and grace. They both shared the desire to wipe away the tension and start anew. Likewise, in our own marriages, when both parties long for reconciliation, it is nearly always possible. But if one party clings to his or her rights and refuses to forgive, reconciliation is very unlikely.

The Shulammite could have said, "I'm sorry I didn't come to the door when you knocked, but it was late. I was expecting you home by seven o'clock. What took you so long anyway? You're partly to blame here too! I have a right to be upset." Of course, Solomon could have argued back with the declaration of his rights. After all, he *was* the king! But clinging to our own rights over God's call to forgiveness and reconciliation never ends well.

I once spent a great amount of time with a friend who was having marriage difficulties. Her husband was absolutely awful. He had anger issues for sure. She had a long list of his shortcomings, and I was ready to string him up by his toenails for the way he was treating his wife. *What a jerk,* I thought.

But later, Steve and I asked him to come to our house and talk about their situation. When he told his side of the story, I was ready to string his wife up by her toenails!

Her conclusion? "Mark has anger issues. I have a right to be hurt."

His conclusion? "Lizzy is always on my case and shows no respect. I have a right to be angry."

Neither one was willing to budge or to consider how they could lovingly relinquish their rights and move toward reconciliation. Self-centeredness had moved into the house and monogrammed its initial on the bathroom towels. After months of counseling, prayer, and intervention by friends who loved them both, the couple divorced.

Oh, girl, unless both husband and wife admit their contribution to the contention and come together with contrition, there will never be reconciliation and healing.

Tommy Nelson wrote:

> Sometimes one spouse will need to abandon "rights" in order to renew or restore the relationship. Each spouse must recognize that individual rights within a marriage are never more important than the unity and love of the relationship as a whole. If in demanding your rights or insisting that you have the right idea or opinion, you

> are threatening to destroy the harmony and loving foundation of your home, you are wrong, no matter how right you think you are. A greater harm is in danger of being done to your marriage and your family by your stubborn resistance than ever could have been done to you personally in the first place.[6]

Relinquishing our rights, particularly in our highly egocentric culture, can be one of the hardest things we ever do. The world constantly screams for individuals to fight for their rights, and it can feel completely counterintuitive not to. "After all," they say, "who's going to stand up for you if you don't stand up for yourself?" But, if anyone was entitled to cling to his rights, it was Jesus. He was fully God and fully man, God's Son, the sinner's Savior. Scripture tells us, "In the beginning was the Word, and the Word was with God, and the Word was God. He was with God in the beginning. Through him all things were made; without him nothing was made that has been made. In him was life, and that life was the light of all mankind" (John 1:1–4). "He committed no sin, and no deceit was found in his mouth" (1 Peter 2:22). And so we have a high priest "who has been tempted in every way, just as we are—yet he did not sin" (Hebrews 4:15).

And what did Jesus do regarding his rights? Paul wrote in his letter to the Philippians:

> In your relationships with one another, have the same mindset as Christ Jesus:
>
> Who, being in very nature God,
> did not consider equality with God something to be used to
> his own advantage;
> rather, he made himself nothing
> by taking the very nature of a servant,
> being made in human likeness.

And being found in appearance as a man,
he humbled himself
by becoming obedient to death—
even death on a cross!

Therefore God exalted him to the highest place
and gave him the name that is above every name,
that at the name of Jesus every knee should bow,
in heaven and on earth and under the earth,
and every tongue acknowledge that Jesus Christ is Lord,
to the glory of God the Father. (Philippians 2:5–11)

"Well, I'm not Jesus," you might say. Nope, that's for sure. You and I are not Jesus. However, if we know him as Savior and Lord, we have the power of the Holy Spirit living in us and working through us to do all things that God has called us to do (2 Peter 1:3). It's up to us to access that power and apply it to our lives. "Nothing will be impossible with God" (Luke 1:37 ESV), but he does require our participation through obedience and faith.

When we crucify our rights on the cross of grace, the resurrection of relationships can become a reality.

All through the Bible, God's power followed man's obedience. Once we make the move toward forgiveness by opening our hands and relinquishing our rights, God's power will follow to make it so. Jesus went to the cross—and the resurrection followed. When we crucify our rights on the cross of grace, the resurrection of relationships can become a reality. I don't want you to think that I've mastered this. Not at all. It's a daily decision and continual struggle. But I do know that the times I *have* followed Christ's example, the rewards have been sweet.

Opening Arms of Grace—Reassuring with Words of Love

Does it bother you when people throw around the phrase "forgive and forget"? The "forgive" part I understand. The "forget" part? That's a conundrum. How can someone wipe the memory of an offense from his or her mind? If there were a delete button on our brains, sure. Having one of those would make life so much easier.

Even Paul talked about forgetting the past. He wrote, "I focus on this one thing: Forgetting the past and looking forward to what lies ahead, I press on" (Philippians 3:13–14 NLT). Paul had been abused and falsely accused by religious leaders who wanted to shut him up and shut him down. And yet he knew that in order to move forward in the cause of sharing the gospel of Jesus Christ, he continually had to forgive those who had beaten him, imprisoned him, and spoken ill of him. He needed to put it behind him and move on.

The Bible says that God forgets our sins and remembers them no more (Jeremiah 31:34). Another conundrum. How does an omniscient God forget? In an effort to try to understand this whole "forgetting" puzzle, I looked up the opposite: what it means when God remembers. It turns out, every time the Bible says, "God remembered," it means that God was about to do something. He remembered Noah, and stopped the rains from coming down (Genesis 8:1). He remembered Rachel, and opened her womb to bear a child (30:22). He heard the children of Israel groaning and remembered his covenant with Abraham, Isaac, and Jacob, so he called Moses to lead the Israelites out of Egyptian slavery (Exodus 2:24). When God chose to forget, the opposite was true; he was not going to act.

When Scripture says that God forgets our sins, it means he is not going to act on them. That I can understand. When we forgive and forget, then, we are choosing no longer to act on the offense or let it act on us.

The other extreme of this type of "forgetting" is keeping a record of wrongs and reviewing the list so that you won't forget, which Paul says is the opposite of love (1 Corinthians 13:5). The termites of refusing to forgive and forget will destroy the foundation of any marriage—especially when the offense is brought up time and time again.

Putting an offense behind you is not sweeping an issue under the rug but putting the issue to rest and burying it in the grave of grace. It's up to you not to dig it up again.

Suppose you are the one who needs to ask forgiveness. Here are some steps to consider:

- Admit what you did or said was wrong.
- Express remorse for the pain you caused.
- Apologize for your actions.
- Ask for forgiveness with the words, "Will you forgive me?"
- Be patient with your spouse if the feelings of forgiveness do not come right away. Give him time to process and heal from the hurt.

We aren't privy to the exact words the Shulammite said to her husband when she found him, but we do see that he opened his arms with grace and forgiveness and never mentioned the incident again. Instead, he began to reassure her with wooing words that melted her heart.

> You are as beautiful as Tirzah, my darling,
>   as lovely as Jerusalem,
>   as majestic as troops with banners.
> Turn your eyes from me;
>   they overwhelm me.

Your hair is like a flock of goats
    descending from Gilead.
Your teeth are like a flock of sheep
    coming up from the washing.
Each has its twin,
    not one of them is missing.
Your temples behind your veil
    are like the halves of a pomegranate.
Sixty queens there may be,
    and eighty concubines,
    and virgins beyond number;
but my dove, my perfect one, is unique,
    the only daughter of her mother,
    the favorite of the one who bore her.
The young women saw her and called her blessed;
    the queens and concubines praised her. (Song 6:4–9)

Once again Solomon elaborated on the Shulammite's beautiful features. He used many of the same words he used on their wedding night, which told her that his love, commitment, and adoration hadn't changed.

Let's break the code and uncover the clues of his romantic reassurances hidden in the poetic language. He began with, "You are as beautiful as Tirzah, my darling." Tirzah was an ancient city located six miles northeast of Shechem. The name meant "pleasure, pleasantness, or beauty." The city was known for its beauty and strength.[7] That's what she was to him.

He also compared her to Jerusalem—the magnificent capital in the south. By comparing her to the exquisite city of Tirzah in the north and to the resplendent capital of Jerusalem in the south, he reaffirmed that she was the most beautiful woman in the entire land.

I love how Peterson paraphrased Solomon's description:

> Your beauty is too much for me—I'm in over my head.
> I'm not used to this! I can't take it in. (v. 5 THE MESSAGE)

I imagine she was giggling with joy at this point. But he wasn't finished! Once again he complimented her on her flowing hair, her dazzling white teeth, and her blushing cheeks. He was so distracted and befuddled by her eyes that he had to turn away from gazing into them so he could think straight. Solomon let her know that, out of all the women in his entire kingdom, she was his dove, his perfect one, unique and one of a kind. In his eyes, there was no one like her.

Unlike his previous recounting of her beauty, Solomon stopped at his wife's face. Perhaps he wanted her to know that this wasn't just about sex. He loved her for who she was, not just what she could give him.

The friends, who had been aware of this marital squabble, were ecstatic that the couple had reconciled.

> Who is this that appears like the dawn,
> fair as the moon, bright as the sun,
> majestic as the stars in procession? (v. 10)

In other words: "Oh, girl, you look absolutely radiant. Your glowing countenance is a far cry from your gloomy face last night. Love looks good on you. Aren't you glad you reached out to your man? We're so proud of you!"

In the next snapshot of the love story, the Shulammite had taken a place of honor in the royal chariot riding among her people—a public display of Solomon's total trust in her (v. 12). She reveled in the assurance that her husband loved her, and they were at peace. The Shulammite received complete forgiveness from her husband, the same kind of forgiveness we want to offer our men.

Celebrating Restoration

In the final words of chapter 6, Solomon's wife was doing a dance for her husband. It was a private party, just for the two of them.

> Why would you gaze on the Shulammite
> as on the dance of Mahanaim? (v. 13)

This was the only time Solomon referred to his wife as "the Shulammite." The name could be a variation of the word *Shunammite*, meaning "a young woman from Shumen," or it could be the feminine form of the word *Solomon*, meaning "Solomon's girl" or "Solomon's counterpart."

So what is the dance of Mahanaim? It all began back in Genesis 25 with the story of Jacob and Esau, two very nonidentical twins. Hairy Esau was Isaac's firstborn, and therefore his father's principle heir. With the help of his manipulative mother, Smooth Jacob stole his brother's birthright and his inheritance. For the next twenty years, Jacob hid from his angry brother. He accumulated wives, children, flocks, servants, and great wealth while living with his father-in-law, Laban. But eventually, Jacob decided he wanted to return to his homeland and his people. There was one problem: Esau.

So Jacob divided his people and possessions into two camps. One was to approach Esau first. If Esau and his four hundred men killed the first wave, then the second group would flee. If Esau didn't kill the first wave, then the second wave would proceed.

When the first camp approached Esau, rather than attack them, he ran to embrace them. The same happened with the second group. When Jacob brought up the rear, Esau embraced his brother, and their relationship was restored. Jacob said that looking into Esau's face of forgiveness was like looking into the face of God. We are never more like God than when we forgive.

This moment was so important in Israel's history that they named the site of reconciliation Mahanaim. In Hebrew, the word means "two camps." Mahanaim would forever remind the Israelite nation of a time when a possible crossfire of animosity became a ceasefire of peace. Jacob and Esau united with tears and dancing after years of hostility. Just the night before, Jacob had been preparing for the worst, but he was met with forgiveness as Esau offered him the best.

After the tension of conflict in Song of Songs 5, Solomon and his Shulammite had come to their place of Mahanaim. The two camps had come together, and all was forgiven. I suspect they would visit Mahanaim many times through the years. Just as my husband and I will. Just as you and your husband will. And each time we will have a choice to turn away from each other and stand our ground in two separate camps, or come together with grace and forgiveness to the rhythm of Mahanaim and the tune of grace.

Chapter 9

The Ageless Beauty of Committed Love

We have a beautiful outdoor fireplace in our backyard. A vine meanders up the back of the stone chimney and surprises us with coral trumpet flowers from spring to fall. Strategically placed variegated bushes snuggle in a bed of pine straw behind a stone wall. Four welcoming Adirondack chairs rest in front of the hearth. Right now yellow mums sit on pillars that bookend the opening. It looks good.

However, and I'm embarrassed to admit it, we seldom strike a match and enjoy a fire in the cool of the evening. What a waste, right? Looking out my workroom window at the pretty view reminds me of a lot of marriages. They look good on the outside, but the fireplace of passion is cold. Oh, friend, I don't want my marriage or your marriage to be like a fireplace that looks pretty on the outside but is cold on the inside. I want us to strike the match, pull up a chair, and enjoy its warmth. I want us to make time for our marriages. Be intentional. Stoke the fire. And add new logs on the flame from time to time. Bring out the s'mores of passion! Do a little roasting! Enjoy the warmth in the seasons of life when a chill hits our bones.

That's exactly what we see happening in the last two chapters of the Song. We get to learn Solomon and the Shulammite's secrets to sexual intimacy and lifelong passion through the passing years. So let's pull up a chair by the hearth and see what we can find out about how to keep the home fires burning for a lifetime.

The Girl's Still Got It

At the beginning of Song of Solomon 7, we find Solomon and his bride in the bedroom . . . again. The years had passed and the topography of their bodies had changed, but their passion had adapted to the graceful aging of the garden delicacies they so enjoyed.

The truth is, you and I might see a woman like the Shulammite walking down the street and not think much about her appearance, but her husband is enthralled with her beauty still. And that's really all that matters. Solomon was that enthralled husband in Song 7, praising his wife's beauty once again.

> How beautiful your sandaled feet,
> O prince's daughter!
> Your graceful legs are like jewels,
> the work of an artist's hands.
> Your navel is a rounded goblet
> that never lacks blended wine.
> Your waist is a mound of wheat
> encircled by lilies. (vv. 1–2)

Yep, the Shulammite's body may have softened, shifted, and even sagged, but Solomon still thought she was the most captivating woman he had ever seen.

I want you to picture him on his knees, holding her feet in his hands, as she sat on the side of the bed. He did not literally worship the ground she walked on, but he certainly loved the feet that did the walking.

Historians point out that only those who were trusted to leave the palace and return again wore sandals. Those who were not trusted, such as slaves and women in harems, were often kept barefoot. The fact that Solomon's wife wore sandals shows that he trusted her implicitly. She could come and go as she pleased. He was not concerned that she would one day walk away and never return. This reminds me of another verse many scholars believe was penned by Solomon's mother about the sort of wife she hoped her son would find: "Her husband has full confidence in her and lacks nothing of value. She brings him good, not harm, all the days of her life" (Proverbs 31:11–12). That's the kind of wife I want to be. I know you do too.

He didn't have to worry that she would embarrass him in public or make fun of him in front of his family and friends. He wasn't concerned that she would keep secrets or hide things from him. If they'd had the Internet, he wouldn't have wondered if she was contacting an old boyfriend or striking up an inappropriate relationship on Facebook. He trusted her with his kingdom. He trusted her with his heart.

After he removed her sandals, Solomon slid his palm up her leg to admire God's handiwork. In his eyes, her legs were graceful—perfectly shaped and alluring. He loved the curves of her calves and the rounded shape of her thighs. She probably had spider veins and cellulite at this point, but he didn't mind or perhaps even notice.

Remember in chapter 1 when Solomon compared the Shulammite to a mare in Pharaoh's chariots? No doubt her legs still reminded him of the graceful horses prancing and galloping through the kingdom. I suspect if he'd had a wallet, Solomon would have had a picture of her legs in his, just as my father-in-law had of Mary Ellen's all those years ago.

In the Old Testament strong legs were a symbol of strong character, of steadfast loyalty and strength. Solomon didn't just praise his wife's beauty but her character as well. Remember what the Shulammite said about Solomon's legs? "His legs are pillars of marble set on bases of pure gold" (Song 5:15). Just as she had admired Solomon's character, he now praised hers. He remembered his mother's words about the type of woman she hoped he would marry: "Many women do noble things, but you surpass them all" (Proverbs 31:29). He had found such a woman.

Solomon moved from admiring his wife's legs to praising her abdomen and surrounding area. He paused to admire and possibly kiss her navel, which he compared to an ever-filled chalice of wine. On their wedding night, Solomon compared the Shulammite's arousal and growing passion to water—first a trickling garden spring, then a deep well of refreshment, and finally a roaring stream from Lebanon. Now he likened her passion to a goblet of blended wine that never ran dry. Just as Jesus changed the water into wine at the wedding ceremony in Cana, the couple's love had changed from water to wine in their later years. It had matured, fermented, and become more flavorful with age. "Your navel is a rounded goblet that never lacks blended wine" (Song 7:2). He was still intoxicated by her body—it would never run dry no matter how old they grew.

Most likely Solomon and the Shulammite had been married for quite some time at this point. We don't know for sure, but there are a few clues, one being the way he lovingly admired her hips and abdomen. "Your waist is a mound of wheat encircled by lilies" (v. 2). No longer was her tummy flat as the desert plains. Time has taken its toll. Perhaps she had given birth to several children. We don't know for sure. But we do know that her tummy had a pooch, and Solomon loved her even more because of it. Perhaps it is what that mound of wheat represented: passing years, bearing of children, maturing love, and enduring passion.

Solomon didn't see his beloved's mound of wheat as a negative. He loved it! And he let her know so. Never once did he speak negatively of physical features. As I've said before, he was a wise man.

Wheat is harvested in the spring; and grapes, which are processed into wine, are harvested in the fall. From the springtime of their lives through the fall and winter, her love satisfied him. From her navel filled with mixed wine to her abdomen like a mound of wheat, her love was the sustenance that fed his heart. He kissed, caressed, and praised once again the gift God had given him in this woman. Perhaps he even nibbled like a gazelle grazing among the lilies. What a picture God has given us of sexual intimacy the way he intended.

Admiring God's Magnificent Masterpiece

Back in Solomon's day women were covered up with full-length robes. No one got to see the Shulammite's shapely legs, graceful arms, or rounded abdomen but her husband. And certainly no one ever saw what was coming next but him.

> Your breasts are like two fawns,
> like twin fawns of a gazelle.
> Your neck is like an ivory tower.
> Your eyes are the pools of Heshbon
> by the gate of Bath Rabbim.
> Your nose is like the tower of Lebanon
> looking toward Damascus. (vv. 3–4)

Solomon stopped to pause at his wife's breasts. This was the same compliment he gave her on their honeymoon (4:5), which makes me like him even more. Those fawns most likely weren't as frisky and perky as they had been those many years ago, but that didn't diminish his admiration or deter his passion. He was still enamored with her seductive sexiness. What woman doesn't want to know that she's still got it after years have morphed youthful beauty into something quite different—that her husband still finds her attractive and alluring? He let her know that he did.

What about that nose? It wasn't a little pug nose. It was "like the tower of Lebanon" (7:4). It's what we might consider . . . large. Oh, friend, we have got to stop allowing our culture to dictate what true beauty looks like. It doesn't get to decide!

Solomon looked into his wife's eyes and compared them to deep pools of water—pools of Heshbon. These were pools in a Levitical city where the priests dwelled. Most likely they ceremonially cleansed themselves in the pools before and after performing certain tasks. Also, the pools were in a desert area, about twenty miles east of the north end of the Dead Sea. Imagine traveling through the hot, dusty desert and coming upon refreshing pools of water. That was what Solomon felt when he looked into his wife's eyes. That is what our husbands can feel when they come home from an arduous day's work . . . if we're intentional. We can be the refreshment they long for after fighting giants in the workplace.

The Shulammite was no longer the timid girl from their wedding night but instead a mature woman who loved deeply and completely. Solomon let her know that she was still just as beautiful now as the first time he saw her. He knew exactly what to say to make her feel secure and where to touch to arouse passion.

No one is harder on a woman's appearance than the woman in the mirror. We can become so self-conscious about what we feel are imperfections, especially as we age. Our insecurities about our naked bodies can put a damper on what should be a fun, carefree, intimacy-building time in the bedroom. But did you know that most husbands have no problem with the areas that their wives consider imperfect? Your husband just likes looking at and enjoying your naked body!

Do you have a mound of wheat rather than a flat plain? Don't worry about that. He loves it. He's not concerned about the cellulite on the back of your legs when you're making love. He's just thinking about how much he loves you and loves loving you.

You are a magnificent masterpiece! Ephesians 2:10 says, "We are God's handiwork." Another translation says, "We are God's masterpiece" (NLT). The Greek word translated "workmanship" or "masterpiece" is *poiema*. It is "a work of masterful creativity, a work of art, or handiwork." *Poiema* is where we get the English word *poem*. The only other time in Scripture Paul used the word was in Romans 1:20: "Since the creation of the world God's invisible qualities—his eternal power and divine nature—have been clearly seen, being understood from *what has been made*, so that people are without excuse" (emphasis added). In that case, it took four English words, *what has been made*, to describe the one Greek word, *poiema*.

God wants you to understand that you are an epic poem. Jon Bloom, staff writer for DesiringGod.org, wrote:

> Tiny, insignificant you are more glorious than the sun and more fascinating than Orion. For the sun cannot perceive its Creator's power in its own blinding glory, nor can Orion trace his Designer's genius in the precision of his heavenly course. But you can. You are part of the infinitesimal fraction of created things that have been granted the incredible gift of being able to perceive the power and native genius of God! And to you, and you only, is given a wholly unique perception and experience of God's holy grand *poiema*. There are some verses God will show only to you. What kind of being are you, so small and weak and yet endowed with such marvelous capacity for perception and wonder?
>
> This is not inspirational poster kitsch. This is biblical reality.[1]

A woman was and is one of God's most magnificent creations. As we've seen before, she was the grand finale of God's creative genius and the inspiration for man's first poetry. Regardless of your self-perceived physical imperfections and the culture-driven definition of your anatomical flaws, you are a magnificent creation of a masterful God. And you are beautiful. As we've also covered, it is difficult for a woman to give herself freely to a man when she feels unattractive. But God wants you to have lifelong intimacy with your husband—one for the history books, or at least your history book. And it begins with seeing yourself as God sees you: stunning.

Romancing the Queen of His Heart

Finally, Solomon got to the top of his wife's head. I imagine it took awhile, as he stopped to enjoy the scenery along the way.

> Your head crowns you like Mount Carmel.
> Your hair is like royal tapestry;
> the king is held captive by its tresses. (Song 7:5)

On their wedding night, Solomon had removed his bride's veil, allowing her hair to fall down and around her shoulders, and likened it to cascading flocks of goats running down the hills of Gilead. On this particular night, he said her hair was like a crown. Queens wore their crowns only at royal and public events. He saw her hair as a perpetual crown worn only for him. She was the queen of his kingdom and the queen of his heart.

I don't think the Shulammite's earlier years were all she'd wished they'd been. At some point her father died, her mother remarried, and her stepbrothers—her mother's sons—made her work in the field under the scorching sun. Life had not been easy. And yet, Solomon assured her that he considered her royalty regardless of her humble beginnings. Sure, she was a queen by marriage, but to her husband, she was royalty long before she moved into the castle.

I don't know what your family was like growing up, but I do know that none are perfect. I grew up in a home riddled with alcohol, violence, and abuse. My parents didn't know how to love their children. I felt that I wasn't, and never would be, good enough to accomplish anything of significance. No matter what you have gone through, your past experiences do not define your present identity. God does. Just as Solomon called his wife a princess, the King of kings calls you his child—his princess.

I love how the *NIV Bible Commentary* summed up Solomon's passionate appraisal of his wife's face and form in chapter 7: "This poem reflects the perpetual charm of the female form to the male. This song has been sung an almost infinite number of times. There is repetition here. Some of his figures are the same as those used in 4:1–15 and 6:4–10. But that is the nature of love. Our language has its limits. Our love pushes those limits and falls back in frustration at the inability of our words to communicate our ecstasy."[2]

That's what we see in Song of Solomon 7. Sometimes there are just not enough words.

I'm not sure what the Shulammite thought of her changing appearance. But I do know that Solomon held up the mirror of his words in hopes that she would see herself through his eyes.

No matter what you have gone through, your past experiences do not define your present identity. God does.

I was having dinner with a group of friends one night, and we were bemoaning our aging bodies with all their wrinkles, crinkles, and sagging parts. One friend in her sixties said, "I'm amazed that my husband still thinks I'm hot! My body is getting saggier by the year, and he still gets excited when I undress in front of him. He still reaches for me in the night." I think the Shulammite felt the same way. She was thrilled that her husband still desired her physically. "I belong to my beloved, and his desire is for me . . . for *me*!" He's still romancing her even though he caught her years ago.

I know we're looking at Solomon's words to his wife in this section, but remember, your husband wants to know that you see him as a masterpiece as well. He wants to know that he's still got it! Picture yourself starting with his masculine calloused feet, which have stood firm for your family, and working all the way up to the crown of his head. He might not have as much hair on that crown as he did when you first married him, and his mound of wheat might be more like a haystack, but he still wants to know that, in your eyes, he is a marvel of masculinity that melts your heart. Go ahead. Give it a try.

Let me say here, several times when I've told women that I'm writing about the Song of Solomon, they've made comments such as, "That man knew how to treat a woman." But, girls, remember this: the Shulammite knew how to treat a man. She showered him with praise and admiration just as much as or more than he did her. If we want a Solomon, then we need to be a Shulammite.

Tasting the Sweet Fruits of Love

Now that Solomon had finished his second rendition of "Head, Shoulders, Knees, and Toes," he told his wife what he was planning on doing with this virtual buffet displayed before him.

> How beautiful you are and how pleasing,
>   my love, with your delights!
> Your stature is like that of the palm,
>   and your breasts like clusters of fruit.
> I said, "I will climb the palm tree;
>   I will take hold of its fruit."
> May your breasts be like clusters of grapes on the vine,
>   the fragrance of your breath like apples,
>   and your mouth like the best wine. (vv. 6–9)

Okay, friend, again, the clusters of fruit are not the Old and the New Testament, as some of the older biblical scholars supposed. Solomon was clearly ready to stop admiring his wife's body and to take hold of all that was his. He compared his wife's breasts to a cluster of dates nestled in the leaves of a palm tree. He was ready to climb that palm tree and take hold of its fruit. It's no wonder that for many centuries Jewish boys were not permitted to read the Song of Solomon.

Pastor J. D. Greear told a story about being in his Bible survey class in the tenth grade. When the class got to the Song of Solomon, the teacher gave a quick summary of the book and then moved on quickly to Isaiah. His curious friend flipped over to 7:7–8 and elbowed J. D. in the side.

"Get a load of this!" he whispered. "Your stature is like that of the palm, and your breasts like clusters of fruit. I said, 'I will climb the palm tree; I will take hold of its fruit.'"

J. D. said their desire to read and know the Bible was transformed overnight![3]

The writers of *The NIV Cultural Background Study Bible* explained more about this tree: "The date palm was (and remains) a highly valued tree in the Near East. It had many uses (e.g., its fronds were used in weaving baskets), and its fruit is sweet. The tree is sometimes associated with fertility goddesses in ancient artwork, and the clusters of its fruit somewhat resemble a woman's breast. As such, it here represents the pleasures that the woman gives."[4]

To Solomon, lovemaking was a feast of delicious dates, intoxicating wine, fragrant apples, and clusters of grapes on the vine. Dates, grapes, apples, and wine were symbolic of the Shulammite's refreshing nourishment to his body, soul, and spirit. She fed his heart emotionally, his body physically, and his inner man spiritually in a way nothing else could. A truly good marriage will have that effect on both husband and wife. That's the way God planned it.

"How beautiful you are and how pleasing, my love, with your delights" (v. 6). Solomon was under his wife's spell—totally captivated.

Serving One Another

We aren't sure how much time had passed since Solomon caught his first glimpse of the Shulammite working in her brothers' field, but we do know that he was still wooing her and pursuing her long after they said "I do." Solomon began chapter 7 by admiring his wife's sandaled feet and slowly moving up to her flowing tresses. His appraisal was very similar to his bouquet of adulation in previous chapters (4:1–7; 6:4–10). However, this time Solomon switched up the order. Earlier, he'd begun at the top of her head and worked his way down. This time he started at the bottom of her feet and worked his way up.

Solomon assumed the position of a servant and took his wife's sandaled feet in his royal hands. He might have been the king of the castle to the outside world, but within the confines of their bedroom, Solomon became the servant stooping low to unfasten his wife's sandals—a job reserved for the lowliest attendants.

During this time in history, it was a servant's job to remove their master's or mistress's sandals. Servants also removed the sandals of honored guests and often washed their feet to remove the dust of travel. With no Reeboks or Nikes, men and women wore leather sandals as they walked the dusty, often muddy, roads of Israel. That's if they had shoes at all. Nothing felt better than to sink calloused, throbbing feet into a cool basin of water and rinse away the cares of the day. Remember when Jesus wrapped a towel around his waist and washed his disciples' feet during the Last Supper?

> It was just before the Passover Festival. Jesus knew that the hour had come for him to leave this world and go to the Father. Having loved his own who were in the world, he loved them to the end.
>
> The evening meal was in progress, and the devil had already prompted Judas, the son of Simon Iscariot, to betray Jesus. Jesus knew that the Father had put all things under his power, and that

> he had come from God and was returning to God; so he got up from the meal, took off his outer clothing, and wrapped a towel around his waist. After that, he poured water into a basin and began to wash his disciples' feet, drying them with the towel that was wrapped around him. (John 13:1–5)

Not all of the disciples were comfortable with Jesus stooping servant-low to wash their feet. Peter balked at the idea of the Christ choosing the towel over the throne. And then, to top it off, as Jesus wiped the last bit of grit and grime from the disciples' feet, he turned and said:

> Do you understand what I have done for you? . . . You call me "Teacher" and "Lord," and rightly so, for that is what I am. Now that I, your Lord and Teacher, have washed your feet, you also should wash one another's feet. I have set you an example that you should do as I have done for you. Very truly I tell you, no servant is greater than his master, nor is a messenger greater than the one who sent him. Now that you know these things, you will be blessed if you do them. (vv. 12–17)

When Jesus washed the disciples' feet, it wasn't simply an act of kindness. He was actually fulfilling a need that they had refused to meet. It was customary for the host of a dinner party to have a servant wash the guests' feet. However, at Jesus' Last Supper with his disciples, no servant was available to wash the guests' feet, and no one volunteered.

So God-made-man wrapped a towel around his waist and did what no one else was willing to do. Jesus did for his disciples what Solomon did for his bride so many years before—he humbled himself to honor another. Solomon tenderly held the Shulammite's sandaled feet in his royal hands and began to unfasten the straps holding them in place. I imagine he even placed a kiss on her toes.

Of course, I am not suggesting that we wash our husbands' feet. Thankfully, we have indoor plumbing these days to take care of that. But we can follow Jesus' and Solomon's examples by serving our spouses in many other ways. We do that every time we do the laundry, cook a meal, clean the house, and a host of other mundane chores. But what about in the bedroom? Have you ever considered that you are honoring God by serving your husband in the bedroom?

We've already talked about the difference between approaching sexual intimacy with the attitude of duty or desire. We've also looked at a third alternative: the decision to love. Making a decision to love—to serve in a way that only you can—honors God and your husband. That is the polar opposite of acting out of duty.

So here's an idea: The next time you feel duty-bound, choose to see sexual intimacy as a way to serve your husband. Not only that, but a *God-ordained* way to serve your husband! Now that's a win-win. I think you'll get so much pleasure out of serving your man in a way that God intended that you'll enjoy sex as never before. As Tim Keller noted, "Sex in a marriage, done to give joy rather than to impress, can change your mood on the spot. The best sex makes you want to weep tears of joy, not bask in the glow of a good performance."[5]

Paul wrote, "Do nothing out of selfish ambition or vain conceit. Rather, in humility value others above yourselves, not looking to your own interests but each of you to the interests of the others" (Philippians 2:3–4). Sometimes it seems easier to think Paul was referring to everyone other than our husbands. However, there's no one more important to apply that principle to than the man we call ours. Whether we are using a telescope to get the big picture or a microscope for close examination, the wise wife pays close attention to her husband's needs, desires, dreams, joys, and sorrows. She looks closely at his heart and thinks of ways to serve him.

But what about husbands? What does the Bible say about his part in serving his wife?

Paul wrote to the Ephesians:

> Husbands, love your wives, just as Christ loved the church and gave himself up for her to make her holy, cleansing her by the washing with water through the word, and to present her to himself as a radiant church, without stain or wrinkle or any other blemish, but holy and blameless. In this same way, husbands ought to love their wives as their own bodies. He who loves his wife loves himself. After all, no one ever hated their own body, but they feed and care for their body, just as Christ does the church—for we are members of his body. "For this reason a man will leave his father and mother and be united to his wife, and the two will become one flesh." *This is a profound mystery*—but I am talking about Christ and the church. However, each one of you also must love his wife as he loves himself, and the wife must respect her husband. (5:25–33, emphasis added)

When Paul said "profound mystery" (NIV) or "great mystery" (NASB), he used the Greek word *mega-mysterion*. Keller called it "an extraordinarily great, wonderful and profound truth that can be understood only with the help of God's Spirit."[6] He also explained,

> [The secret of marriage] is the message that what husbands should do for their wives is what Jesus did to bring us into union with himself. . . . Jesus *gave himself up* for us. Jesus the Son, though equal with the Father, gave up his glory and took on our human nature (Philippians 2:5ff). But further, he willingly went to the cross and paid the penalty for our sins, removing our guilt and condemnation, so that we could be united with him (Romans 6:5) and take on his nature (2 Peter 1:4). He gave us his glory and power and became a servant. He died to his own interests and looked to our needs and interests instead (Romans 15:1–3). Jesus's sacrificial service to

> us has brought us into a deep union with him and he with us. And *that*, Paul says, is the key not only to understanding marriage but to living it. . . . Do for your spouse what God did for you in Jesus, and the rest will follow.[7]

Serving doesn't mean the bondage of slavery. As Jesus put on the towel and served his disciples, he proved conclusively that God's kind of serving love flows from choice, not coercion; from strength, not weakness; from gladness, not guilt.

What stands in the way of serving our husbands as Jesus so beautifully demonstrated? One word: *self.* When "we" becomes "me," when what I want becomes more important than what my husband wants, the strands of the intertwined relationship begin to unravel. Keller wrote, "The result is always a downward spiral into self-pity, anger, and despair, as the relationship gets eaten away to nothing."[8] Putting others before yourself isn't thinking less of yourself; it is thinking of yourself less.

To make a marriage sing, as we're seeing in the Song of Solomon, we must take ourselves off the throne and put the needs of our spouses above our own. Sound impossible? I think it is . . . if left to our own ability to do so. That's why we need the power of the Holy Spirit to do it through us.

> To make a marriage sing, we must take ourselves off the throne and put the needs of our spouses above our own.

Jesus said, "Give, and it will be given to you. A good measure, pressed down, shaken together and running over, will be poured into your lap. For with the measure you use, it will be measured to you" (Luke 6:38). In most cases, when you give selflessly to your husband, he will give to you in return. However, it may be entirely possible for you to serve your husband and feel you are not receiving anything in return. That's when you remember that your heavenly Father is always watching. The measure you use to bless your husband, your Father will use to bless you in return.

Responding with Enthusiasm

What would you do if your husband approached you the way Solomon approached his wife in chapter 7? What would I do? The Shulammite didn't miss a beat. At his words, "May your breasts be like clusters of grapes on the vine, the fragrance of your breath like apples, and your mouth like the best wine," she responded eagerly and expectantly.

> May the wine go straight to my beloved,
> flowing gently over lips and teeth.
> I belong to my beloved,
> and his desire is for me. (Song 7:9–10)

"Bring it," she teased. "I'm all yours!"

Want to make your husband really happy? Nothing turns your man on more than knowing that he has turned *you* on. Let him know that he still excites you—that his touch still sends shivers down your spine. Then watch him smile. I bet Solomon grinned from ear to ear.

In verse 10 the Shulammite used the Hebrew word *teshuqah*, which is translated "desire." It occurs only two other times in the Bible, both in Genesis. It can mean "sexual desire" or "a desire to control," as when God spoke to Eve in Genesis:

> "I will make your pains in childbearing very severe;
> with painful labor you will give birth to children.
> Your desire will be for your husband,
> and he will rule over you." (Genesis 3:16)

In the garden of Eden, after Adam and Eve disobeyed God and ate the forbidden fruit from the Tree of the Knowledge of Good and Evil, the harmony of marriage was turned to discord—the symphony of intimacy to the cacophony of competition and strife. But here, and only here, the Shulammite alluded to the harmony restored: "I belong to my beloved and his desire, his pure and holy desire, is for me." The desire she spoke of mirrors what God had intended all along—no control, no strife, naked and unashamed.

Keller wrote, "Sex is perhaps the most powerful God-created way to help you give your entire self to another human being. Sex is God's appointed way for two people to reciprocally say to one another, 'I belong completely, permanently, and exclusively to you.'"[9] That's what the Shulammite was saying to her man. "After all these years, I still desire you! You still desire me! I can't wait to make love to you—to feel your hands move over the palm tree and to drink in the wine of your kisses."

The Shulammite delighted in giving him pleasure just as he delighted in receiving it. And here's the key: she let him know it. You need to let your husband know that you delight in his touch, and that you delight in giving him pleasure as well. This is how God planned it.

The poet Percy Bysshe Shelley wrote, "Soul meets soul on lovers' lips."[10] This is not just about having sex. This is about the intertwining of souls for a lifetime of covenantal intimacy. "I am my beloved's and his desire is for me" is the chorus to each stanza of a hug, a kiss, an embrace, a coming together as one. It is the covenant renewed each time we come together as man and wife.

Craig Glickman wrote about the Shulammite, "Her body is a passionate instrument, playing a song of love from her heart to his." [11] The sound of the instrument mellowed and sweetened with time, especially when the couple made sure to keep it tuned with intentional romance.

Chapter 10

Keeping Romance Alive with Intentionality and Ingenuity

Why is it that passionate romance routinely fizzles out over the years? Why does a soulmate so easily become a roommate? Why does the rapid heartbeat of excitement in the early years morph into the heavyheartedness of disappointment in the later years?

There are many reasons why passion cools, and we've already looked at a few. But passion in marriage doesn't have to fizzle out with the passing years. That certainly isn't God's plan. He has a much different desire for your marriage and mine. Yes, sexual intimacy will change as we grow older. Hormones wane. Libido lessens. Stamina decreases. Bodies don't always cooperate. That's a given. But I believe intimacy can grow and mature into something sweeter, deeper, and more profound than any clothes-ripping frantic frenzy ever could be.

I mentioned my outdoor fireplace in the last chapter. Here's something I've noticed when we do actually use it: It only takes a little bit of kindling, a few wads of paper, and one match to ignite a fire. However, it requires diligent effort to keep the fire going. To have a steady flame, you have to add logs to the fire when it starts to die down, poke the wood so the charred ash falls off and new sparks fly, and sometimes fan the flame so it will burn brighter. Sounds a lot like what we've learned about maintaining lifelong intimacy. Left on its own, a fire or a marriage won't flourish but turn to ash. It takes intentionality and ingenuity to make lifelong intimacy a reality.

It happens to every couple—the monotony of matrimony. Kids' schedules, long workdays, piles of bills, mounds of laundry, never-ending housework, and the grass that needs cutting every single week! It is so easy to collapse into bed each night, give each other a quick peck on the cheek, and click off the bedside lamp . . . only to get up the next day and do it all over again. Who has the mental capacity to be creative in the bedroom? Who has the energy to be spontaneous? Who has time to break from the routine for a date night? Who has the energy to make lovemaking a priority after doing all that we have to do on any given day? I'll tell you who. A smart woman who knows that strong marriages don't just happen. They take a lot of work. Marriages that sing with intimacy that lasts a lifetime are intentional, purposeful, and playful.

Left on its own, a fire or a marriage won't flourish but turn to ash. It takes intentionality and ingenuity to make lifelong intimacy a reality.

The Shulammite was a wise woman who took deliberate action that left nothing to chance. I envision her in the next stanza sauntering up to her husband as he's overseeing the fields. She whispered in his ear, and her warm breath teased his neck. Tempting him. Flirting with him still.

> Come, my beloved, let us go to the countryside,
> let us spend the night in the villages.
> Let us go early to the vineyards
> to see if the vines have budded,

if their blossoms have opened,
and if the pomegranates are in bloom—
there I will give you my love.
The mandrakes send out their fragrance,
and at our door is every delicacy,
both new and old,
that I have stored up for you, my beloved. (Song 7:11–13)

In chapter 1 Solomon came bounding over the hills, coaxing the Shulammite to come away and enjoy the spring day with him. Now she was coaxing him to steal away to spend some alone time with her. No doubt Solomon had been busy running the kingdom, overseeing his land, and ruling his people. Just like all married couples, they needed to get away for some time by themselves. I can just picture her tugging on his robe and pulling him away from his work.

"Come, my *dodi*," she coaxed. "Let's go to the countryside like we used to. Let's spend the night in one of those quaint little cottages where no one knows who we are or where we are. We can open the windows and enjoy the scent of the henna blossom wafting on the breeze. I will give you my love, and you can enjoy my garden." Then she winked and coyly teased, "I have the old fruit that you enjoy so much, and I even have some new fruit—a few new tricks up my sleeve—that I think you'll enjoy as well."

The Shulammite is very intentional with the words she used to entice her husband. Glickman noted:

> Her teasing play on words is as creative as the lovemaking she promises, provocatively revealing her desire to entice Solomon to come with her. At our doors, she says, are erotic fruits. But the word for *doors* is also the word for *openings*, a variation in the form she has used to describe the opening of blossoms in the previous lyric. She

> uses this term instead of the more common one for *door* so she can give it an erotic double meaning. But she also infuses it with beauty, having just used it to portray the opening of flowers in spring. It's a lovely depiction of her sexuality—blossoms unfolding, revealing treasures of delicious fruit.[1]

I don't think it took too long for Solomon to change his schedule, cancel his meetings, and pack his bags.

The Shulammite mentioned pomegranates again—those seed-filled symbols of lovemaking and fertility in the ancient world. She also mentioned mandrakes. An enormous amount of lore and superstition was associated with the mandrake plant in the ancient times (Genesis 30:14–16). It had a pungent scent much like ginseng and was considered an aphrodisiac. The shape of the root resembled human form. The word *mandrake* literally means "love plant" and was thought to help women conceive.[2] Walter and Keener wrote, "In Egyptian artwork, women hold the fruit under their noses or the noses of their husbands, apparently as a preparation for love-play."[3] It might be like you or me waving a scented piece of lingerie under our husbands' noses. In light of the folklore that surrounded the mandrakes, Solomon would have known that his wife was not suggesting a stroll through the produce stand in the marketplace.

Traditionally, men are seen as the aggressors or initiators and women the recipients or responders, but did you know that your husband dreams about your being the initiator as well? When I surveyed men for a previous book, they let me in on a little secret. They dream about their wives initiating intimacy—not all the time, but occasionally. What this says to your husband is, "I want you!"

In this case, Solomon's wife was the initiator. Was their lovemaking tedious and monotonous, as some suppose love in the later years is bound to be? Absolutely not. It certainly could have been. But she made sure it was neither stale nor stodgy.

That is not to say that every time a husband and wife comes together in physical intimacy it has to be off-the-charts exciting. That certainly isn't realistic. But a wise couple does make time for a "gourmet meal" every now and then.

What if you're just not as interested in romance and physical intimacy as you used to be? What do you do about that? I think of it like this: When I first became a Christian, I was so in love with Jesus! No one ever had to tell me to read my Bible, pray, or make sure I was in fellowship with other believers. I would have been happy as a peach to stop everything and simply focus on my relationship with Jesus.

However, with time, some of that enthusiasm waned. Daily life threw cold water on spiritual fervor. I knew that in order to have a maturing relationship with Jesus, I needed to establish some disciplined times of Bible reading and prayer, get plugged in to a local church, and have accountability. I didn't love Jesus any less than the first day I met him, but our relationship changed, at least on my part. I had to be intentional to keep the relationship strong.

It's the same way with a husband and wife. Remember, marriage is a physical example of a spiritual relationship with Christ. If we have to practice certain disciplines to grow and mature in our relationship with our heavenly bridegroom, then it only makes sense that we would have to do the same with our earthly bridegroom.

In chapter 7 the Shulammite is taking the initiative, inviting her husband to come away for some time alone. It wasn't even their anniversary or Valentine's Day, just a beautiful spring weekend.

Prioritizing Your Relationship

Great marriages don't just happen. They take a lot of work. As we've seen, some of that "work" is a lot of fun. As I noted earlier, there is no mention of children throughout the entire Song of Songs. I think that's important; this love song is about the two of them. They've laid aside their roles as parents and focused on their roles as lover and friend. I think grandma Bathsheba did a lot of babysitting, especially for their nights away.

It's crucial for a couple to keep their marriage a priority. Years ago a woman with children who didn't have an outside job was called a *housewife*. Now that same woman is called a *stay-at-home mom*. Some might think that's a good change. Who wants to be married to their house, right? But here's the tragedy. Rather than focusing on being a wife, the focus has shifted to being a mom, and marriages have suffered because of it.

When I was growing up, my parents didn't even like each other. The atmosphere vacillated between heated arguments and passive-aggressive coolness. I would have given anything to know that my parents loved each other. Knowing that Mom and Dad love each other and make their relationship a priority is something that gives a child security and confidence more than almost anything else parents can do. So remember to keep your marriage a priority. Do it for your husband. Do it for your kids.

If you have young children and money is tight, trade off babysitting with another couple. If you can't afford to go away for the weekend, send the kids away to stay with friends or relatives. Hello, Grandma! A good goal is to have a date night once a week and an extended time away at least once a year. Children need to know that Mom and Dad have certain times that they spend together, just the two of them. They might not understand when they are little, but, believe me, they will be so glad you did when they are older. Not only that, you will be modeling the proper way for married couples to build and maintain a strong relationship.

Even today, my grown son brags about his parents' strong relationship. "I'm glad you guys hugged and kissed around me when I was growing up," Steven once told me. "I was actually proud of you guys and your relationship when so many of my friends didn't have that as a foundation in their home. I was sad for them."

Sometimes your husband wants you all to himself. He might not tell you, but he does! He needs to know that you can take off the mommy hat and give him your full attention. I can still remember the first time Steve and I went away by ourselves and left one-year-old Steven at home with Grandma. I cried a few times when Steve wasn't looking. It was hard at first. But the weekend did wonders for Steve. He needed to know that he was still the king of my heart, even though that little prince took up so much of my time. We've made sure to have at least one weekend away each year since, and that was more than thirty-five years ago.

If you're empty nesters and are home alone every night anyway, that doesn't count. A date night needs to be time away from the home to reconnect and have fun. There's more to getting away as a couple than romance—it's also about deepening your friendship and simply having a good time together.

Relishing the Sweetness of Aging Intimacy

You've seen it. So have I. You're watching a movie or television program when a man and a woman catch each other's eye. Before the sixty minutes are up, they're ripping each other's clothes off and having passionate sex, usually standing up against a wall. But that's not the reality of lifelong intimacy.

Christian sex therapists Joyce and Clifford Penner assure us:

> Those initial high-drive desires are fueled by the brain chemical dopamine, which is a powerful motivator or driving energy. As the brain production of dopamine decreases, the couple needs to shift to an attachment fueled more by the brain chemical oxytocin.

> Oxytocin, which is associated with bonding, is released during hugging and pleasant physical touch, and plays a part in the human sexual response cycle. This oxytocin-fueled attachment is deeper, binding love that lasts a lifetime. Yet the shift from large doses of dopamine to this oxytocin-fueled connection can feel like a loss.
>
> Be assured: Desire isn't gone, it is just different. Nor have you lost your attraction to or love for each other. That also is just different! Embrace and enjoy the shift to a softer, more subtle urge for closeness and touch. After fifty-three years of marriage, we can promise you it is wonderful![4]

Here we go getting scientific again. But isn't it amazing to see how God has engineered the human body to work, even well into our older years? This is his plan!

Here's something that might surprise you. When the National Health and Social Life Survey completed an extensive survey of Americans' sex lives, they found:

1. Sexually active singles have the most sexual problems and get the least pleasure out of sex.
2. Men with the most "liberal attitudes about sex" are seventy-five percent more likely to fail to satisfy their partners.
3. Married couples by far reported the happiest satisfaction with their sex lives.
4. The most sexually satisfied demographic group of them is that of married couples between fifty and fifty-nine![5]

Fifty and fifty-nine? Yep. Intimacy grows sweeter with time.

As a husband and wife grow old together, some aspects of lovemaking will change. A man's testosterone peaks in his midtwenties and then decreases 1 percent every year. After menopause, a woman's libido lessens and her vaginal walls become drier and thinner. There are ways to remedy both of these situations, but the point is, our bodies change. It is the perceptive husband and wise wife who are attuned to what brings pleasure as these changes occur and are then intentional about bringing satisfaction and joy.

A nurse who worked in a nursing home commented about an elderly couple in her care:

> Two of the people who live in this particular home have been married to each other for seventy years. They are both in their nineties now, and they get around in wheelchairs. The casual visitor might think they are weak and frail and beyond any feelings of sexual desire. But you should see how they look at each other! They may not share a common bed, but they still hold hands and kiss and flirt with each other in a way that can almost make a person feel embarrassed to watch them. There is no doubt they are still very much in love and that the feelings they have for each other are sexual as well as emotional. They still have the hots for each other.[6]

No doubt Solomon and the Shulammite's relationship in chapter 7 was very different from their relationship on their wedding day in chapter 4. They weren't elderly by any means but older for sure. Like a couple who has been dancing together for years, there is an intermingling that becomes almost second nature. Steve and I have been literally dancing together for more than thirty-eight years. It is easy to follow his lead. He lifts his arm; I spin under. He applies a slight pressure on the small of my back; I come in closer. He steps back; I pull away. But that didn't come naturally. We didn't "move as one" the first time we took to the dance floor. The fluidity of motion and ease of grace came with time and practice.

People often talk about the magic of the honeymoon night, but the real magic comes much later. The longer a couple is married, the more comfortable they become. The awkwardness gives way to confidence as each learns what the other enjoys and how their bodies respond. The wine of lovemaking grows sweeter with the years. The garden grows to be abundant with ripened fruit. Inexperience gives way to comfort and ease.

Such is the beauty of maturing love as lovers morph to the rhythm of change, like shape-shifters keeping pace with aging topography and ageless hearts.

Such is the beauty of maturing love as lovers morph to the rhythm of change, like shape-shifters keeping pace with aging topography and ageless hearts.

My in-laws were such a couple. They were a walking duet synchronized to the melody of tender devotion. I remember watching them on their sixtieth wedding anniversary in a dimly lit restaurant surrounded by children and grandchildren. Faces lined with years embraced cheek-to-cheek, weathered hands and arthritic fingers interlaced, and a slow-but-steady pace served as a picture of enduring love that spanned over half a century. Bruce pulled out Mary Ellen's chair for her to take her seat; Mary Ellen brushed a crumb from Bruce's wrinkled cheek. He poured water in her glass; she added cream to his coffee. Still loving. Still serving. Still lovestruck in the winter of their lives. Every husband and wife's dream.

Chapter 11

Unquenchable, Unstoppable, Unsurpassable Love

I want you to think for a moment. What do you want the last few years of your marriage to look like? To feel like? To be like? Right now, today, you are making it what it will be down the road. Shaping it. Molding it. Word by word, you're writing your history. Your present will one day be your past, and the marriage you will celebrate in the future is being formed today.

The truth for all of us is that we don't know when the last few years will be. No matter our age, we could be spending the last few years now. Solomon and his Shulammite have given us a beautiful portrait of what a marriage can be. Is it entirely perfect? Not by a long shot. Is it enduringly strong? Absolutely. But we've not yet seen the complete picture. Song of Songs 8 adds a few finishing touches.

The final chapter of the Song is a bit strange in that it seems like a collection of snippets looking back and moving forward. We'll find some of the key elements of romance, marriage, and lifelong intimacy, plus a final word on implementing them on our own journeys. It's as if the Shulammite were saying, "I know I need to close this song, but there are a few things I really want you to remember. So let's go back to the beginning and review, and then look ahead to the future."

Remember, the Song was written in a chiasm like a folded letter. In many ways chapter 8 mirrors chapter 1. She started the song with a kiss and concluded by placing a kiss on the final page.

> If only you were to me like a brother,
>   who was nursed at my mother's breasts!
> Then, if I found you outside,
>   I would kiss you,
>   and no one would despise me.
> I would lead you
>   and bring you to my mother's house—
>   she who has taught me.
> I would give you spiced wine to drink,
>   the nectar of my pomegranates. (Song 8:1–2)

Back in Solomon's day husbands and wives weren't allowed to show public displays of affection, especially kissing. They weren't even permitted to hold hands or give a quick hug beyond the walls of their home. However, a girl could kiss her brother or father for all the world to see without a hint of judgment. I'm sure the Shulammite didn't really wish Solomon were her brother, but she certainly did wish that she didn't have to limit their kisses to the privacy of their own home.

In the movie *Sweet Home Alabama*, there's a flashback to when the two main characters, played by Reese Witherspoon and Josh Lucas, are about ten years old. The young boy asked the wide-eyed girl to marry him.

"Why would you want to marry me for anyhow?" she asked him back.

"So I can kiss you anytime I want," he replied with a grin.[1]

That's what the Shulammite was lamenting. She wished she could kiss her man anytime she wanted.

When she mentioned "spiced wine . . . the nectar of my pomegranates" in verse 2, she was letting Solomon know that she wasn't thinking about a brotherly kiss. He would have known exactly what she was alluding to. Oh, girl, she was still speaking in code and flirting with her man. This reminds us never to stop.

My husband loves it when I grab his hand in public, give him a peck on his cheek when we're with friends, or simply touch his leg when we're riding in the car. Those small signs of affection let him know that I love him and always put a smile on his face. Aren't you glad that we don't live with the rules the Shulammite did but can kiss our men anytime we want?

Take a look at the action words in these two verses. "If I *found* you . . . I would *kiss* you. . . . I would *lead* you and *bring* you. . . . I would *give* you . . ." Each phrase drew him closer and closer to the physical intimacy she was teasing him with. I imagine the rapid pace of the words and the urgency they implied made his heart skip a beat. Just as the single Shulammite flirted with Solomon in chapter 1, the married Shulammite flirted with him again in chapter 8. It's clear that this is important. Don't stop romancing your husband. Don't stop letting him know that he has captured your heart—that you'd marry him all over again. She started the Song that way and ended the same. "If only you were my brother and I could kiss you anytime I want, I'd give you spiced wine to drink . . . and well, you know what comes next."

Then her flirting took a seductive turn.

> His left arm is under my head
> and his right arm embraces me. (v. 3)

A more literal reading of the original Hebrew would be, "His left arm *should be* under my head and his right arm *should* embrace me" (emphasis added).[2] What she dreamed about in 2:6 could now be a reality. Her sensual flirtation had moved to erotic desire. Remember from 2:6, the Hebrew word used here for *embrace* actually means "to clasp or hug, fondle or stimulate with gentle stroking."[3] Once again, the words of the song are desirous but discreet. She wasn't shy about letting her husband know she still found him alluring and wanted to be intimate with him. She left no room for doubt. She was also modeling the intentionality of lifelong romance for us. Just because we grow older doesn't mean that our passion has to grow colder.

Remembering the Beginning

My Grandma Edwards was a countrywoman who worked hard and loved long. She had six children on the heels of the Depression. Her husband died when her youngest, my dad, was five years old. I loved spending time with this resiliently rugged and tenderly tenacious woman. She could cut a switch from the willow tree with one hand and cut you a piece of apple pie from the larder with the other.

Grandma had a large garden with various fruit trees in her backyard. I remember her picking apples and singing a song made popular by the Andrews Sisters during World War II, "Don't Sit Under the Apple Tree (with Anyone Else But Me)."[4] The lyrics are about two young lovers who pledged their enduring love while one of them is away serving in the war.

I wonder if Grandma Edwards thought of her husband when she picked those apples from the tree. I wonder if she was singing those words to my grandpa, letting him know that she was thinking of him, even though they would never sit under that apple tree on this side of heaven again.

The apple tree was also a special place for the Shulammite and her *dodi*. It reminded her of the early courting days of chapter 1 when they sat under the tree in the open field. Under the tree is where Solomon wooed her—where Solomon won her.

Under the apple tree I roused you;
there your mother conceived you,
there she who was in labor gave you birth. (v. 5)

Back in chapter 2 the Shulammite said he was like an apple tree among all the other trees of the forest. While commentators aren't exactly clear on her meaning in chapter 8, it is clear that the apple tree held special memories for them.

Perhaps she was telling Solomon that she believed his mother conceived him just for her. I was born ten months after my husband. We always tease that as soon as he was born, God began fashioning me just for him. I don't think I was conceived under an apple tree, but it is fun to think I was created just for Steve. By mentioning the apple tree at the end of the song, I believe the Shulammite was thinking back to the early days of their blossoming romance.

Isn't that what anniversaries are all about? Remembering the beginning? One of the most common commands in the Bible is, "Remember," because we are so prone to forget. We remember the joys of our budding beginning to shore up our marriage's middle and help us press on to leave a lasting legacy of enduring love.

As I mentioned earlier, marriage is an earthly example of a heavenly relationship between Christ and the church. We read in the New Testament that the church at Ephesus was a good church. God applauded their perseverance, endurance, and discernment. And yet, at some point they lost their fire for the Father. He told them, "I hold this against you: You have forsaken the love you had at first" (Revelation 2:4). Perhaps that describes your marriage. Perhaps you've persevered over

We remember the joys of our budding beginning to shore up our marriage's middle and help us press on to leave a lasting legacy of enduring love.

the years, but now there's not much passion. Maybe your marriage has become a bit lukewarm. God has a fix for that. He told the Ephesian church, "Consider how far you've fallen! Repent and do the things you did at first" (v. 5). In other words, "Remember, and return." Remember the things you did at first. Return and do them again.

Making a Decision to Love for a Lifetime

I remember when my eighty-two-year-old father-in-law was taken by ambulance to the emergency room. When my slow-moving mother-in-law finally arrived sometime later, the nurse said, "I don't know who you are, but I sure hope your name is Mary Ellen!"

Yes, their gaits were slow, but their connection was immediate. As soon as she walked in the room he calmed down. She reassured him with her words, kissed his weathered cheek, and held his crippled hand. They shared a love that lasted their lifetimes, the kind that doesn't wane when years pass and circumstances change.

That is what we see with Solomon and the Shulammite. Their covenant of marriage was for keeps.

> Place me like a seal over your heart,
> like a seal on your arm;
> for love is as strong as death,
> its jealousy unyielding as the grave.
> It burns like blazing fire,
> like a mighty flame.
> Many waters cannot quench love;
> rivers cannot sweep it away.
> If one were to give
> all the wealth of one's house for love,
> it would be utterly scorned. (Song 8:6–7)

The Shulammite asked that he place her like a seal over his heart and on his arm. A seal was an official mark of identification placed on a letter or document. It was created by dripping soft wax on folded paper and imprinting the wax with a stamp. The seal indicated authorship, ownership, authenticity, and protection—and not ownership in a demeaning way but in endearing devotion. The Shulammite longed to be an imprint on Solomon's heart, a permanent impression. Just as he was like the pouch of myrrh resting between her breasts in chapter 1, she was like a seal that rested over his heart in chapter 8.

Today, we exchange wedding rings. The ring says to the world, "I belong to my husband and he belongs to me . . . for as long as we both shall live." The Shulammite welcomed that kind of "ownership." She had given herself to her man, just as he had given himself to her. "I am my beloved's and my beloved is mine" (6:3). This was no passing fancy that could be shrugged off if the feelings wore off. They were committed to each other no matter what. The couple had established their commitment on their wedding day when they made a covenant before God.

Our culture hasn't prepared us for the waxing and waning of feelings. "He's not the same man I married twenty years ago," I hear women say. Well, thank God for that! We all change. The man you marry on your wedding day will not be the same man twenty, thirty, or even fifty years later. And you will not be the same woman. The trick is to bend, flex, and adapt as your spouse grows, changes, and matures—to make sure you're growing together.

Richard Seltzer shared his experiences as a surgeon in his book, *Mortal Lessons: Notes on the Art of Surgery*. In one of his most poignant essays, he told of a young woman with a tumor in her cheek. In order to excise the tumor, Seltzer was forced to cut a tiny but important nerve that controlled the muscles on one side of her mouth. The woman was scarred for life, her face slightly droopy on one side, her smile crooked.

I stand by the bed where a young woman lies, her face post-operative, her mouth twisted in palsy, clownish. A tiny twig of the facial nerve, the one to the muscles of her mouth, has been severed. She will be thus from now on. The surgeon had followed with religious fervor the curve of her flesh; I promise you that. Nevertheless, to remove the tumor in her cheek, I had to cut the little nerve.

Her young husband is in the room. He stands on the opposite side of the bed, and together they seem to dwell in the evening lamplight, isolated from me, private. Who are they, I ask myself, he and this wry-mouth I have made, who gaze at and touch each other so generously, greedily? The young woman speaks.

"Will my mouth always be like this?" she asks.

"Yes . . . because the nerve was cut."

She nods, and is silent. But the young man smiles.

"I like it," he says. "It is kind of cute."

All at once I *know* who he is. I understand, and I lower my gaze. One is not bold in an encounter with a god. Unmindful, he bends to kiss her crooked mouth, and I am so close I can see how he twists his own lips to accommodate to hers, to show her that their kiss still works.[5]

Again, in love that lasts a lifetime, lovers morph to the rhythm of change, like shape-shifters keeping pace with aging topography and ageless hearts.

The Beauty of Giving Love

The Shulammite we see in chapter 8 is not the same insecure girl we met in chapter 1. She had grown up. And she was still committed to her marriage and her man.

Yes, marriage is meant to last a lifetime, and we can make the decision every day to commit to this kind of love. The word translated as "love" in 2:5, 5:8, and 8:6–7 is the Hebrew word *ahava*, and it means "to have affection, sexually or otherwise, to like, to befriend, to be intimate." It is a love of the will or act of doing, more than just a fleeting feeling. The root word is *ahav* and means "to give." *Ahava* is a giving love. When she used this word, the Shulammite was more concerned with giving than receiving—one of the keys to lifelong intimacy. "Giving love" creates and sustains romantic love.

Too often people say they "fell in love" and then "fell out of love." You don't fall in or out of love as if it were an accidental stumbling. The cessation of love grows out of a thousand small decisions *not to love*, taking steps that move the heart farther away from the one once loved. If that is the case, we can take steps back toward the one once loved by practicing *ahava*—giving love.

Studies show that "86 percent of unhappily married people who stick it out find that, five years later, their marriages are happier." In fact nearly 60 percent of those who rated their marriage as unhappy and stayed married rated their same marriage "very happy" or "quite happy" when reinterviewed five years later.[6] In comparison, those who divorced and remarried divorced again at a rate of 60 percent.[7] Sometimes making a decision to love, regardless of how you feel on any particular day, is the first step toward taking the next step, and the next, and the next. Sometimes successful marriages happen because two people keep showing up and continue working it out.

Our God doesn't just create; he re-creates. No matter what your marriage has been in the past, you can start today to make it better. The good news is, you are never alone. God is always right there with you. He can make a bad marriage good, and a good marriage great. It's never too late to start anew.

God can even take a valley of dead, dry bones and raise them up to be a powerful army (Ezekiel 37:1–14). If he can do that, he can certainly resurrect dead marriages. The word *hopeless* is not in God's vocabulary. His giving love gives us hope no matter how difficult our circumstances may be.

There will be times when one spouse has nothing to give. That's when giving love bridges the gap and loves for both. Charlie Wedemeyer experienced giving love with his wife, Lucy.

Charlie was a college football coach when he was diagnosed with ALS—Lou Gehrig's disease. The doctors gave Charlie one year to live, but he fooled them all and lived twenty-two. He even coached football for seven more years after his initial diagnosis. Coaching kept his mind sharp, helped him to focus on something bigger than himself, and provided an opportunity for him to give back to others. He felt that if he couldn't coach, he would lose one of his biggest reasons for living. So Lucy set about helping him continue on. When he could no longer walk, Lucy drove him up and down the sidelines in a golf cart. When he could no longer talk, Lucy read his lips and relayed his coaching instructions.[8]

Lucy tried to encourage Charlie as best she could, but after a championship loss, his spirits were as hard to prop up as his weakening body. One afternoon his assistant coach stopped by for a visit. Lucy was just about to bring him to the bedroom to see Charlie when Charlie stopped her.

"No," he told her. "I'd rather go out to the living room."

Before he headed out to see his friend, Charlie stopped by the bathroom. I'll let Charlie's words tell you the rest of the story:

> She held me tight and we began a tediously slow shuffle into the bathroom. We were barely through the door when I began to cough. My knees buckled and I would have crashed to the floor if Lucy hadn't instantly tightened her grip on my arm and wedged me against the wall with her body. I felt her muscles strain and tried to stiffen my legs to help, but with each cough I could feel another bit of strength seep from my body. When the first spasm

of coughing passed, it was all Lucy could do to move me over and ease me onto the seat.

At that moment, I sensed the utter futility of my life. While thoughtful friends waited nearly an hour in the living room to see me, and my exhausted, loving wife stood watching over me, I sat hopelessly on a [toilet] seat, too weak to move and too discouraged to keep on fighting.

Tears of humiliation and frustration welled up in my eyes as I looked up at Lucy, sighed in resignation and said what I'd felt was true for a long time: "You and the children would be better off if I died."

I'll never forget Lucy's reaction. Later I learned my words had so startled her that she silently prayed, "Please God, give me the words to say." Slowly, deliberately, she straightened up as she gathered her thoughts and looked right at me. In an almost angry, don't-you-forget-it tone tempered by the love in her eyes, she said, "We would rather have you like this, than not have you at all."

I was suddenly overcome by emotion, overwhelmed by the love of this woman who had already been through so much with me. I'd never in my life felt so loved by her. I began to sob. She put her arms around me and we sobbed together. And after a time we regained enough composure and strength to get to the living room for a short visit with our guests.

I had no idea how long I would continue to live. But I knew I'd never forget Lucy's words that day. What I didn't know was how many times the memory of those words would help keep me alive by giving me the will to continue fighting for my next breath.[9]

Lucy's words to Charlie were the air he breathed. Her giving love literally sustained him through the trying, painful years that followed. Charlie explained, "I drew more strength from Lucy's positive reaction than I could ever understand, let alone express."[10]

That's giving love. Love when sexual intimacy is an impossibility. Love when one party has nothing to give in return. Love when one person has to breathe for the other. This is what "for better or worse" is all about. It is a love that says, "I'm not going anywhere."

The way the Shulammite described this *ahava* love was "as strong as death," relentless as the grave. She also called it a "blazing fire" and "a mighty flame," which literally means "like the very flame of the Lord" or "the flame of God." This kind of love is permanent, and it can warm you for a lifetime.

How intense and enduring is that flame? She said that many waters cannot quench it; rivers cannot sweep it away. Even in the rising tides of turmoil and the swift currents of contention, giving love is the anchor that keeps a marriage sure.

The Shulammite also said that *ahava* love is priceless. Solomon's mama taught him this same lesson: "An excellent wife who can find? She is far more precious than jewels" (Proverbs 31:10 ESV). As Solomon's wife, the Shulammite had access to more money than any woman in the ancient world, and yet she understood that no amount of money could buy *ahava* love. If someone suggested that it could, they would be laughed out of the house. *Ahava* love is freely given and freely received. You can't put a monetary value on it. There's only one price to be paid, and Jesus showed us that on the cross. The price for *ahava* love is the gift of oneself. We give love freely, and the return on that investment is invaluable. Giving love is the best love of all.

Taking a Final Bow

Remember the Shulammite's brothers back in the fields? We haven't heard anything about them since chapter 1. At the conclusion of the Song, we see something like a curtain call inviting the brothers to come onto the stage to take a final bow.

We have a little sister,
and her breasts are not yet grown.
What shall we do for our sister
on the day she is spoken for?
If she is a wall,
we will build towers of silver on her.
If she is a door,
we will enclose her with panels of cedar. (Song 8:8–9)

The brothers remembered when the Shulammite was a young girl whose body had not yet begun to bloom. They may have seemed tough on her by making her work in the fields, but they also made sure that she stayed in a locked-up garden until the time was right. Her purity was secured by their protection, like towers built to protect the city walls. Maybe they were good guys after all. She grew to think so.

I am a wall,
and my breasts are like towers.
Thus I have become in his eyes
like one bringing contentment.
Solomon had a vineyard in Baal Hamon;
he let out his vineyard to tenants.
Each was to bring for its fruit
a thousand shekels of silver.
But my own vineyard is mine to give;
the thousand shekels are for you, Solomon,
and two hundred are for those who tend its fruit.
(vv. 10–12)

Solomon owned the vineyards where the Shulammite and her family worked in earlier days. They were simply tenants. And while she originally thought her stepbrothers harsh for making her work in the scorching sun, she now appreciated how they cared for her in difficult times. "And two hundred are for those who tend its fruit," she said with a nod toward her stepbrothers. I'll be honest, I didn't like those guys very much in the beginning, but now I would love to give them a hug of gratitude.

As we know, the Shulammite's body didn't stay a wall forever. She blossomed into a beautiful woman who captured Solomon's heart, who brought him contentment and satisfaction as no one else could. While Solomon owned the vineyards her family tended, he did not own her. She gave her vineyard to him willingly and completely. Then he became the one tending her garden, and he enjoyed its delicious fruits until the end of their days.

We don't know how old Solomon and his Shulammite were at the close of their love song. Part of me wants to believe they were old and gray, slow of gait but still quick of mind. With a twinkle in his eye, Solomon offered last words that echoed his desire from their courting days. He beckoned his precious wife to come to him. He longed to see her face and hear her voice as he wooed her still.

> You who dwell in the gardens
> with friends in attendance,
> let me hear your voice! (v. 13)

The Shulammite responded in kind by inviting her *dodi* to run to her as a gazelle on the spice-laden mountains. She began the Song with her desire for her lover's kisses and ended it with her longing for more passionate love.

> Come away, my beloved,
> and be like a gazelle
> or like a young stag
> on the spice-laden mountains. (v. 14)

The love song closes with a declaration of mutual desire between two lovers, implying that love goes on.

I can just picture the lights on the stage grow dim and the lovers reach for each other's hand.

They smile at us, the grateful crowd.

They take their final bow.

The Song of Solomon . . . the Greatest of All Songs.

Writing Your Love Song

I could hear the wailing from the driveway. It was 5:10 a.m. and nature soundly slept. All was quiet, except for the animallike cries making their way out the back door and into the still dark dawn. My husband and his sister were giving their mom the news that her husband of sixty years had passed away. After three months in a rehab facility recovering from a fall, Bruce Jaynes quietly slipped away and took Jesus' hand.

Jesus or no Jesus, Mary Ellen was devastated that her husband had left her.

"How could he leave me?" she cried through salty tears. "He said he wouldn't leave me."

They had been a matched set. Like a candlestick made to be part of a pair whose mate had gone missing, her light was exponentially dimmer without her Bruce.

In the following months Mary Ellen walked with the limp of a woman missing half of herself. Her forced smile looked pained. It was difficult to watch as two intertwined souls became a single strand. Four grown children and their spouses, plus a slew of grandchildren and great-grandchildren, took extra care to let her know that she was loved and needed, but it was never enough. Six months after Bruce took his last breath, Mary Ellen joined him. After a fun-filled day at a great-grandchild's birthday party, she had a heart attack and left us in a matter of minutes.

Bruce's Shulammite had gone to be with her *dodi*. I could almost hear her whispers as he came for her . . .

> Listen! My beloved!
>   Look! Here he comes,
> leaping across the mountains,
>   bounding over the hills.
> My beloved is like a gazelle or a young stag.
>   Look! There he stands behind our wall,
> gazing through the windows,
>   peering through the lattice.
> My beloved spoke and said to me,
>   "Arise, my darling,
>   my beautiful one, come with me." (Song 2:8–10)

And she did.

I think of Mom Jaynes as we come to the end of these pages. I think of how she would've loved to pick up Bruce's dirty socks from the bedroom floor one more time. How she would've given anything to hear him blowing his nose too loudly in front of company. How she would've happily ironed his shirts yet again, or heard his snoring instead of silence in the night. How she would've much rather cooked a meal for two than heat up a bowl of soup for one.

What would she say to those women who teeter on the brink of divorce, who huff in frustration, who turn their backs to their husbands' reaching hands in the night? I think she would hold their gaze with a knowing look. Grasp their hands with an urgent plea. I think she would tell them that marriage is worth fighting for. It's worth the hurt and the healing. The ups and the downs. The irritations and the celebrations.

I think she'd tell them that the big picture of marriage is created with the brushstrokes of tiny moments—that both the dark and the vibrant hues are necessary for depth and beauty to emerge. That the marriage of two imperfect people is the perfect recipe for God's glory to manifest itself to a longing world. That the legacy of a lifetime is too precious to toss away. Work at it. Give it all you've got. Start over as many times as you have to, as long as it's with the same man. The best marriage you will ever have is the one you have right now.

> The marriage of two imperfect people is the perfect recipe for God's glory to manifest itself to a longing world.

She would remind us that marriage isn't all about you and me. It's about glorifying God. It's about sacrifice. It's about caring for the needs of someone else above your own. It's about believing in the impossible when your hope is all but gone. It's about asking God to give you wisdom and then having the courage to change when he reveals the problem is you. It's about a covenant with the God who intertwines two souls with the thread of his presence.

I think she would say to forgive quickly and completely. Don't waste one day on bitterness or resentment. Because time is precious and fleeting, and when it's gone, it's gone. All you have is today.

Breaking the Secret Code for Song of Solomon

Much of the Song of Solomon is written in what I call "secret code." Of course, to the readers of Solomon's day, the words would have made perfect sense. But for the modern reader, the comparisons are rather foreign and require a bit of sleuthing to discover their meaning. The following is a key to help decipher the code and grasp the beauty of the poetic language.

1:5 *Tents of Kedar*—Arab nomadic tribal tents woven from black goat hair

1:5 *Tent curtains of Solomon*—most likely the beautiful dark curtains of Solomon's palace

1:6 *My own vineyard*—the Shulammite's own body; her personal appearance or complexion

1:7 *Veiled woman*—wandering about as one blindfolded (most likely not referring to the veiling of a prostitute)

1:13; 4:6; 5:13 *Myrrh*—"A low, thorny, ragged-looking tree, something like an acacia. . . . a viscid white liquid oozes from the bark when punctured, which rapidly hardens when exposed to the air, and becomes a sort of gum, which in this simple state is the myrrh of commerce"[1]

1:14; 4:13 *Henna*—a flowering shrub with fragrant white blossoms still found today only at En Gedi; produces yellow, orange, and red dye, which was used to color the hair and other parts of the body

1:14 *En Gedi*—a lush oasis just west of the Dead Sea, meaning "fountain of the king"

1:15; 4:1; 5:12 *Dove eyes*—beautiful, deep, smoke-gray eyes of the dove

2:1 *Rose of Sharon*—a bulb flower like a crocus, narcissus, iris, or daffodil growing in the fertile watered areas; an ordinary flower (definitely not a rose as we know it)

2:1, 16 *Lily of the Valley*—possibly a six-petal flower that grew in the fertile watered areas. Lotus flowers were symbols of fertility and sensuality in Egypt and Canaan.

2:4 *Banqueting house*—literally "house of wine"; not actually a banquet hall but "the place of the delights of love"[2]

2:4 *Banner*—a military banner or standard used as a symbol of possession, raised when a land was conquered

2:5 *Raisins*—a food associated with a religious festival, having possible erotic significance; metaphor for love's caresses and embraces

2:9 *Gazelle*—often portrayed as the companion of the goddess of love in ancient Near Eastern art; celebrated for its form and beauty

2:14; 5:2; 6:9 *Dove*—a shy bird that mates for life; a common symbol of love

2:17 *Mountains of Bether*—a ravine or rugged hills that separate two areas in an unidentifiable location in Israel

3:3; 5:7 *Watchmen*—guards who patrolled the city at night and stood sentry at the city gates and on the city walls

3:7, 9 *Couch, palanquin, litter*—a sedan chair that transported the king and his bride

4:1; 6:5 *Mount Gilead*—a high plateau east of Galilee and Samaria

4:1; 6:5 *Flock of goats*—long-haired black goats whose hair would blow in cascading motion as they ran down the hills of Mount Gilead

4:2; 6:6 *Sheep just shorn*—newly shorn sheep that are clean and still moist with water coming out of washing

4:3, 13; 6:7, 11; 7:12 *Pomegranate*—a round, red, seeded fruit that often represented fertility and lovemaking

4:4 *Tower of David*—an armory tower of King David; represented the pride and glory of a city (Long necks, like a tall well-built tower, were seen as beautiful in the ancient Near East.)

4:4 *A thousand shields*—phrase referring to warriors' practice of decorating towers with shields, as a woman's neck was decorated with jewels and/or necklaces[3]

4:8 *Amana, Senir, Hermon*—landmarks of the area; neighboring peaks or perhaps different names for the same peak,; symbolizes rough places

4:9, 10, 12; 5:1, 2; 8:8 *Sister*—term of endearment in the ancient Near East

4:13–14 *Henna, Nard, Saffron*—most likely spices that Solomon would bring from the Far East (along with calamus and cinnamon), symbolizing the sweetness, attractiveness, and value of his bride

4:14 *Myrrh and Aloes*—aromatic aloes used to perfume royal nuptial robes.

5:14 *Chrysolite (Beryl)*—possibly a yellowish or greenish stone such as topaz

5:14 *Sapphires Azure*—blue lapis

6:4 *Tirzah, Jerusalem*—two beautiful, magnificent cities in Israel located seven miles northeast of Shechem in Samaria.

7:4 *Pools of Heshbon*—pools in the city in Transjordan, east of the Dead Sea, now called Tell Hesban; serene and calm

7:5 *Mount Carmel*—a wooded mountain in northern Israel
7:5 *Royal tapestry*—purple royal cloth
7:7 *Palm tree*—highly valued tree in the Near East, which fronds were used for weaving baskets and the sweet fruit for eating; sometimes associated with fertility goddesses in ancient artwork; fruit clusters somewhat resemble a woman's breast[4]
7:13 *Mandrakes*—fruit with a pungent scent similar to ginseng and considered an aphrodisiac; associated with fertility; can be used as a narcotic; has root that can resemble a human form[5]
8:1 *Brother*—term of endearment a woman would use for her lover in ancient Near East
8:6 *Seal*—typically a piece of clay with a stamp on it that identified the owner of whatever was sealed; as personal as a person's name
8:11 *Baal Hamon*—location unknown; *baal* means "lord," *hamon* sometimes means "wealth" or "abundance"; possibly meaning of "lord of abundance" referring to Solomon's wealth[6]

Acknowledgments

The inspiration for *Lovestruck* occurred years ago. As I watched my husband's parents live a lifetime of committed, covenantal love, I wanted that for myself, for my son, and for the women I would have the opportunity to lock arms with in the years to come. Thank you Mom and Dad Jaynes for teaching by example what forever love looks like.

My deepest gratitude goes to: my agent, Bill Jensen, who always wants the best for me; my editor, Jessica Wong, who pushes me to make good words great; and the Proverbs 31 First 5 Team who ignited the spark in me to dig deeper into The Song of Solomon. A special thanks also goes to my prayer team who prayed me through the process; and my Girlfriends in God, Mary Southerland and Gwen Smith, who've put up with all my shenanigans for more than a decade; and Brooke Martinez who keeps me organized and "socialized."

Most importantly, I am forever grateful for my precious husband, Steve—my *dodi*, my beloved for life.

Notes

Introduction

1. Paul Suggett, "Does Sex Really Sell in Advertising?" The Balance Careers, last modified December 29, 2018, https://www.thebalance.com/does-sex-really-sell-38550.
2. Linda Klepacki, "What Your Teens Need to Know About Sex," Purity Series, Focus on the Family, 2005, https://www.focusonthefamily.com/lifechallenges/love-and-sex/purity/what-your-teens-need-to-know-about-sex.
3. *ABC News*, "Porn Profits: Corporate America's Secret," http://abcnews.go.com/Primetime/story?id=132001&page=1.
4. Abigail Geiger and Gretchen Livingston, "8 Facts About Love and Marriage in America," Fact Tank, Pew Research Center, February 13, 2019, http://www.pewresearch.org/fact-tank/2019/02/13/8-facts-about-love-and-marriage/.
5. Ligonier Ministries, "The Song of Solomon," https://www.ligonier.org/learn/devotionals/song-solomon/.
6. Richard S. Hess, *Song of Songs* (Grand Rapids, MI: Baker Academic, 2005), 70.
7. Watchman Nee, *The Song of Songs: The Divine Romance Between God & Man* (Anaheim, CA: Living Stream Ministry, 1993), 63.
8. Timothy Keller with Kathy Keller, *The Meaning of Marriage: Facing the Complexities of Commitment with the Wisdom of God* (New York: Penguin Books, 2013), 254.
9. Keller and Keller, 253.
10. Kenneth L. Barker and John R. Kohlenberger III, *Zondervan NIV Bible Commentary, Volume 1: Old Testament* (Grand Rapids, MI: Zondervan, 1994), 1027.

Chapter 1: The Mystery of Physical Attraction

1. Craig Glickman, *Solomon's Song of Love: Let the Song of Songs Inspire Your Own Romantic Story* (West Monroe, LA: Howard Publishing, 2004), 40.
2. C. S. Lewis, *The Four Loves* (New York: Harcourt Brace, 1960), 158.
3. Hess, *Song of Songs*, 50 (see intro., n. 6).
4. Sheril Kirshenbaum, "The Science of Kissing," CNN, February 14, 2012, http://www.cnn.com/2012/02/14/opinion/kirshenbaum-science-kissing/index.html.
5. Emil Ludwig, *Of Life and Love* (1945, reprint, Garden City, NY: Blue Ribbon Books, 1946), 29.
6. Quoted in Andréa Demirjian, *Kissing: Everything You Ever Wanted to Know About One of Life's Sweetest Pleasures* (New York: Penguin Group, 2006), 12.
7. Research and Markets (website), "Perfume Market: Global Industry Trends, Share, Size, Growth, Opportunity and Forecast 2019–2024," February 2019, https://www.researchandmarkets.com/reports/4752278/perfume-market-global-industry-trends-share.
8. Elizabeth Svoboda, "Scents and Sensibility," *Psychology Today*, January 1, 2008, https://www.psychologytoday.com/us/articles/200801/scents-and-sensibility.
9. Tommy Nelson, *The Book of Romance: What Solomon Says About Love, Sex, and Intimacy* (Nashville, TN: Thomas Nelson, 1998), 5.
10. John H. Walton and Craig S. Keener, eds., *NIV Cultural Backgrounds Study Bible: Bringing to Life the Ancient World of Scripture*, (Grand Rapids, MI: Zondervan, 2016), 1089.

Chapter 2: The Deepening of Desire

1. *The Brown-Driver-Briggs Hebrew and English Lexicon*, s.v. "rayah," https://www.biblestudytools.com/lexicons/hebrew/nas/rayah.html.
2. Ellen F. Davis, *Proverbs, Ecclesiastes, and the Song of Songs* (Louisville, KY: Westminister John Knox, 2000), 247.
3. *Same Kind of Different as Me*, directed by Michael Carney, written

by Michael Carney, Alexander Ford, and Ron Hall, based on book with same title written by Ron Hall and Denver Moore with Lynn Vincent (Hollywood, CA: Paramount Pictures, 2017), https://www.springfieldspringfield.co.uk/movie_script.php?movie=same-kind-of-different-as-me.

4. Sheldon Vanauken, *A Severe Mercy*, (New York: HarperOne, 2009), 35.
5. Vanauken, 36.
6. Glickman, *Solomon's Song of Love*, 60 (see ch. 1, n. 1).
7. Anne Lamott, quoted in Rick Reed, *Good Stuff for Your Heart & Mind: A Book of Quotes*, 2nd ed., (self-pub, 2016), 264.
8. Hess, *Song of Songs*, 73.
9. Ed Wheat and Gaye Wheat, *Intended for Pleasure*, 2nd ed. (Old Tappan, NJ: Fleming H. Revell, 1981), 83.
10. Dennis F. Kinlaw, *Song of Solomon* in *The Expositor's Bible Commentary*, vol. 5, ed. Frank E. Gaebelein, (Grand Rapids, MI: Zondervan, 1991).
11. Levi Lusko, *Swipe Right: The Life-and-Death Power of Sex and Romance* (Nashville, TN: Thomas Nelson, 2017), xxiii.
12. Lusko, 198.
13. Joe Carter, "(Almost) Everyone's Doing It," First Things, September 27, 2011, https://www.firstthings.com/blogs/firstthoughts/2011/09/almost-everyones-doing-it.
14. Samuel Taylor Coleridge, *Coleridge on Shakespeare: The Text of Lectures of 1811–12*, ed. R. A. Foakes, 2nd ed., (Oxford, UK: Routledge, 2005), 86.
15. Lewis, *Four Loves*, 71 (see ch. 1, n. 2).

Chapter 3: Little Foxes and Pesky Fears

1. J. Allan Hobson, "REM Sleep and Dreaming: Towards a Theory of Protoconsciousness," *Nature Reviews Neuroscience* 10, no. 11 (November 1, 2009): 803–13, abstract, http://www.nature.com/articles/nrn2716.
2. Glickman, *Solomon's Song of Love*, 87.

Chapter 4: Saying "I Do" and Meaning "I Will"

1. Maggie Seaver, "The National Average Cost of a Wedding Hits $35,329," The Knot, https://www.theknot.com/content/average-wedding-cost-2016.
2. Hess, *Song of Songs*, 109.
3. Nelson, *The Book of Romance*, 81 (see ch. 1, n. 9).
4. Francis Brown, et al, *The Brown-Driver-Briggs Hebrew and English Lexicon*, (Peabody, Mass.: Hendrickson Publishers, 1906), s.v. "dabaq," https://www.biblestudytools.com/lexicons/hebrew/nas/dabaq.html.
5. Bradley R. E. Wright, *Christians Are Hate-Filled Hypocrites . . . and Other Lies You've Been Told: A Sociologist Shatters Myths from the Secular and Christian Media* (Bloomington, MN: Bethany House, 2010), 133.
6. David McLaughlin, The Role of the Man in the Family (audio series), quoted in Philip C. McGraw, *Relationship Rescue: A Seven-Step Strategy for Reconnecting with Your Partner* (New York: Hyperion, 2000), 247. The series is available at Discipleship Library: www.discipleshiplibrary.com.
7. Mike Mason, *The Mystery of Marriage: Meditations on the Miracle* (Colorado Springs, CO: Multnomah, 1985), 81.
8. Matt Chandler with Jared C. Wilson, *The Mingling of Souls: God's Design for Love, Marriage, Sex & Redemption* (Colorado Springs, CO: David C. Cook, 2015), 101–102.
9. Chandler and Wilson, 102.
10. C. S. Lewis, *The Weight of Glory, And Other Addresses* (New York: Macmillan, 1965), 5.

Chapter 5: Unlocking the Secret Garden

1. "I'm Gonna Do Beautiful Things for You," written by Toni Wine and Barry Mason, performed by The Embers on track 13 of *25th Anniversary*, 1994, https://www.allmusic.com/album/25th-anniversary-mw0000039615.
2. Glickman, *Solomon's Song of Love*, 22.
3. Michael V. Fox, *The Song of Songs and the Ancient Egyptian Love Songs*

(Madison, WI: University of Wisconsin Press, 1985), 131. As quoted in Hess, *Song of Songs*, 134.

4. Nelson, *The Book of Romance*, 92.
5. Mason, *The Mystery of Marriage*, 37 (see ch. 4, n. 7).
6. Mason, 113.
7. J. D. Greear, "Approaching Marriage Healthy," April 13, 2008, Exposed sermon series, The Summit Church, https://www.summitrdu.com/message/approaching-marriage-healthy/.
8. Bill and Pam Farrel, *Men Are Like Waffles—Women Are Like Spaghetti* (Eugene, OR: Harvest House Publishers, 2001), 48.
9. Nelson, *The Book of Romance*, 89.
10. Kevin Leman, *Sheet Music: Uncovering the Secrets of Sexual Intimacy in Marriage* (Carol Stream, IL: Tyndale House Publishers, 2002), 52.
11. Leman, 11.
12. Glickman, *Solomon's Song of Love*, 32.
13. J. D. Greear, "Let's Talk About Sex Again, Baby," April 27, 2008, Exposed sermon series, The Summit Church, 18:00, https://www.summitrdu.com/message/lets-talk-about-sex-again-baby/.
14. Lusko, *Swipe Right*, 24 (see ch. 2, n. 11).
15. C. S. Lewis, *Mere Christianity*, rev. ed. (New York: HarperOne, 2009), 104.
16. Chandler and Wilson, *The Mingling of Souls*, 133 (see ch. 4, n. 8).

Chapter 6: Trouble in Paradise

1. Stu Weber, *Four Pillars of a Man's Heart: Bringing Strength into Balance* (Colorado Springs, CO: Multnomah, 1997), 269.
2. Keller and Keller, *The Meaning of Marriage*, 8 (see intro., n. 8).
3. Joy Davidson, "So Your Relationship's Honeymoon Phase Is Over? Here's the Surprising Good News," Dr. Joy Davidson (website), http://joydavidson.com/portfolio/so-your-relationships-honeymoon-phase-is-over-heres-the-surprising-good-news/.
4. Nelson, *The Book of Romance*, 97.
5. Juli Slattery, "When Your Husband Isn't Interested in Sex," Focus on the Family (website), https://www.focusonthefamily.com/marriage

/sex-and-intimacy/when-your-husband-isnt-interested-in-sex/when-your-husband-isnt-interested-in-sex.

6. Shaunti Feldhahn, *For Women Only: What You Need to Know About the Inner Lives of Men* (Colorado Springs, CO: Multnomah, 2004), 111–12.
7. Feldhahn, 112.
8. Feldhahn, 113.
9. Feldhahn, 114.
10. George Gilder, *Men and Marriage* (Gretna, LA: Pelican Publishing, 1986), 73.
11. Jill Renich, *To Have and to Hold: The Feminine Mystique at Work in a Happy Marriage* (Grand Rapids, MI: Zondervan, 1972), 55.
12. Rob Flood, "5 Communication Tools That Saved My Marriage," Family Life (website), 2005, http://www.familylife.com/articles/topics/marriage/staying-married/communication/5-communication-tools-that-saved-my-marriage.

Chapter 7: This Is My Beloved, This Is My Friend

1. Sharon Jaynes, *Becoming the Woman of His Dreams*, 2nd ed., (Eugene, OR: Harvest House, 2015), 193.
2. Jaynes, 197.
3. Jaynes, 202.
4. William Barclay, *The New Daily Study Bible: The Letter to the Hebrews*, 3rd ed. (Louisville, KY: Westminster John Knox Press, 2002), 145–46.
5. Andy Stanley as quoted by Ann Wilson, "Affirming Your Man," interview by Dennis Rainey and Bob Lepine, The Power of a Woman's Affirmation series, *FamilyLife Today*, June 24, 2015, http://familylifetoday.com/program/affirming-your-man/.
6. John Eldredge, *Wild at Heart: Discovering the Secret of a Man's Soul*, rev. ed. (Nashville, TN: Thomas Nelson, 2010), 60–62.
7. *The Brown-Driver-Briggs Hebrew and English Lexicon*, s.v. "rayah," https://www.biblestudytools.com/lexicons/hebrew/nas/rayah.html.
8. John M. Gottman and Nan Silver, *The Seven Principles of Making*

Marriage Work: A Practical Guide from the Country's Foremost Relationship Expert, rev. ed. (New York: Harmony, 2015), 19.

9. Sheldon Vanauken, quoted in William and Nancie Carmichael, comp., *601 Quotes About Marriage and Family* (Carol Stream, IL: Tyndale, 1998), 80.

Chapter 8: Forgiveness and the Dance of Two Camps

1. Ruth Graham, quoted in Gayle Haggard, *Courageous Grace: Following the Way of Christ* (Carol Stream, IL: Tyndale, 2013), 133.
2. Chandler and Wilson, *The Mingling of Souls*, 157.
3. Terry Gaspard, "How Forgiveness Can Transform Your Marriage," The Gottman Institute, December 29, 2016, https://www.gottman.com/blog/forgiveness-can-transform-marriage/.
4. Spiros Zodhiates, ed., *The Complete Word Study Dictionary: New Testament* (Chattanooga: AMG Publishers, 1992), 229.
5. Rick Warren, *The Purpose Driven Life: What on Earth Am I Here For?* (Grand Rapids, MI: Zondervan, 2002), 179–80.
6. Nelson, *The Book of Romance*, 129–30.
7. Hess, *Song of Songs*, 200; *Archaelogical Study Bible*, (Grand Rapids, MI: Zondervan, 2005), 1044

Chapter 9: The Ageless Beauty of Committed Love

1. Jon Bloom, "You Are God's Workmanship," Desiring God, May 11, 2015, http://www.desiringgod.org/articles/you-are-god-s-workmanship.
2. Barker and Kohlenberger, *Zondervan NIV Bible Commentary*, 1034 (see intro., n. 10).
3. J. D. Greear, "Laws of Attraction," March 30, 2008, Exposed sermon series, The Summit Church, 2:34, https://www.summitrdu.com/message/the-laws-of-attraction/.
4. Walton and Keener, *NIV Cultural Backgrounds Study Bible*, 1097 (see ch. 1, n. 10).
5. Keller and Keller, *The Meaning of Marriage*, 83.
6. Keller and Keller, 41.
7. Keller and Keller, 41–43.

8. Keller and Keller, 56.
9. Keller and Keller, 257.
10. *The Poetical Works of Percy Bysshe Shelley*, ed. Harry Buxton Forman, (London: Reeves and Turner, 1882), 2:450.
11. Glickman, *Solomon's Song of Love*, 127.

Chapter 10: Keeping Romance Alive with Intentionality and Ingenuity

1. Glickman, *Solomon's Song of Love*, 134.
2. Antonio Escohotado, *The General History of Drugs*, vol. 1, trans. and ed. G. W. Robinette (Valparaiso, Chile: Graffiti Militante Press, 2010), 127.
3. Walton and Keener, *NIV Cultural Backgrounds Study Bible*, 1098.
4. Joyce J. Penner and Clifford L. Penner, *Enjoy! The Gift of Sexual Pleasure for Women* (Carol Stream, IL: Tyndale, 2017), 9.
5. Danny Akin, *God on Sex: The Creator's Ideas about Love, Intimacy, and Marriage* (Nashville, TN: B&H Publishing, 2003), 162.
6. Nelson, *The Book of Romance*, 166.

Chapter 11: Unquenchable, Unstoppable, Unsurpassable Love

1. *Sweet Home Alabama*, directed by Andy Tennant, written by C. Jay Cox and Douglas J. Eboch (Burbank, CA: Touchstone Pictures, 2002), http://www.script-o-rama.com/movie_scripts/s/sweet-home-alabama-script-transcript.html.
2. Interlinear Bible, "Song of Solomon 8," BibleHub, http://biblehub.com/interlinear/songs/8.htm.
3. Wheat and Wheat, *Intended for Pleasure*, 83 (see ch. 2, n. 9).
4. "Don't Sit Under the Apple Tree (with Anyone Else But Me)," written by Sam Stept, Lew Brown, and Charles Tobias, performed by The Andrews Sisters on track 4 of *Songs That Won the War: Something to Remember You By*, 1999, https://play.google.com/music/preview/Texdxjps3mzv5nl54pc7qsfswmy?play=1.
5. Richard Selzer, *Mortal Lessons: Notes on the Art of Surgery* (New York: Simon & Schuster, 1974), 45–46.

6. Linda J. Waite and Maggie Gallagher, *The Case for Marriage: Why Married People Are Happier, Healthier, and Better Off Financially* (New York: Doubleday, 2000), 148.
7. Judith S. Wallerstein, Julia M. Lewis, and Sandra Blakeslee, *The Unexpected Legacy of Divorce: The 25 Year Landmark Study* (New York: Hyperion, 2000), 295.
8. Charlie and Lucy Wedemeyer with Gregg Lewis, *Charlie's Victory: An Autobiography* (Grand Rapids, MI: Zondervan, 1993).
9. Wedemeyer, 174–76.
10. Wedemeyer, 62.

Breaking the Secret Code for Song of Solomon

1. Andrew Harper, ed., *The Cambridge Bible for Schools and Colleges* (Cambridge: Cambridge University Press, 1902), https://biblehub.com/commentaries/cambridge/songs/1.htm.
2. Charles John Ellicott, ed., *A Bible Commentary for English Readers* (London: Cassell and Company, 1905), https://biblehub.com/commentaries/ellicott/songs/2.htm.
3. Nelson, *The Book of Romance*, 92.
4. Walton and Keener, *NIV Cultural Backgrounds Study Bible*, 1097.
5. Antonio Escohotado, *The General History of Drugs*, 127 (see ch. 10, n. 2).
6. Kenneth L. Barker, ed., *NIV Study Bible* (Grand Rapids, MI: Zondervan, 1985).

About the Author

Sharon Jaynes has been encouraging and equipping women through ministry for more than twenty-five years. She served as vice president and radio cohost of Proverbs 31 Ministries for ten years and currently writes for their online devotions, Encouragement for Today and First 5 Bible study app. Sharon is also an international conference speaker, author of more than twenty books, and the cofounder of Girlfriends in God, Inc. She has been romancing her husband, Steve, for thirty-eight years, and they make their home in Weddington, North Carolina.